Applied Differential Games

Applied Differential Games

Alexander Mehlmann
University of Technology
Vienna, Austria

Plenum Press • New York and London

Library of Congress Cataloging in Publication Data

Mehlmann, Alexander.
Applied differential games.

Includes bibliographical references and index.
1. Differential games. I. Title.
QA272.M44 1988 519.3 88-15248
ISBN 0-306-42897-0

A Division of Plenum Publishing Corporation
233 Spring Street, New York, N.Y. 10013

Printed in the United States of America

To Grace, my dearest opponent,
and Sabrina, our cooperative outcome

Preface

This book grew out of a set of lecture notes for a one-semester course on dynamic game theory held at the University of Technology, Vienna. It is intended primarily at the graduate level for students in operations research, management science, applied mathematics, and economics. I hope that I have been able to give the reader an accessible introduction to the subject of nonzero-sum differential games with particular emphasis on applications.

It would be irrational to try to reach total comprehensiveness in a single volume. Therefore, I have resisted the temptation to "over-cannibalize" previous textbooks and monographs on the subject. It has rather been my desire to cover material that (I think) is important and interesting, but gets left out of these publications.

Writing a book is quite a game. In the beginning—before closing the *binding agreement** with Plenum—I believed this to be a *finite horizon* game. Time, however,

* Key words will be explained in the text.

was a merciless arbiter. I am grateful to the Senior Editor, Dr. Ken Derham, for allowing manuscript delivery to become a (restricted) *free terminal time* problem.

Most of all, I thank my wife Grace for offering me the needed spiritual support, and my two-year-old daughter Sabrina for ignoring the paradoxical situation that there are games which prevent Dad from playing with her.

The Department of Operations Research (under Professor Gustav Feichtinger's mild *Stackelberg leadership*) ensured *playability* of the game's actions. Access to *information* has been made possible by a grant (S 3204) from the Austrian Science Foundation.

In reading many preliminary versions, Gerhard Sorger provided an invaluable and *perfect feedback* of the state of the game. I am also grateful to my student Mr. Horst Holzweber who (by producing the drawings) made the game illustrative. Richard F. Hartl taught me that we are living in a *tragedy of the commons* world (by simultaneously using scarce resources such as paper, printer, and personal computers).

During the last stages of manuscript preparation, I deliberately engaged in an extreme version of a *zero sum* differential game—*kendo*, the art of Japanese fencing; hopefully an *efficient* and *credible threat* in any future game of refereeing.

Alexander Mehlmann

Vienna

Contents

1. Introduction 13
1.1 The Glass Bead Game 15
1.1.1. Isaacs's Decade 16
1.1.2. The Aftermath 17
1.2. Dynamic Models of Conflict 18
1.2.1. A Compact with the Devil 18
1.2.2. A Game of Capitalism 21
1.2.3. Strike Negotiation 23
1.2.4. A Model of Duopolistic Competition 24
1.2.5. The Competitive Limited-Access Fishery 25
1.3. Symbols and Terminology 26
1.3.1. Notation 26
1.3.2. Related Terms 29

2. Playing the Game 35
2.1. Rules of the Game 37
2.1.1. Basic Definitions 37
2.1.2. The Loop Model 40
2.1.3. Generalized Concepts 44

2.2. The Noncooperative Approach 49
2.2.1. Equilibria of (Normal Form) Actions 49
2.2.2. Strategic Features 64
Exercises 71

3. Methods of Solution 73
3.1. Simultaneous Play 75
3.1.1. Sufficiency under Generalized Constraints 77
3.1.2. Necessary Conditions under Generalized Constraints 82
3.2. Hierarchical Play 96
3.2.1. Equilibria in Two-Person Games 96
3.2.2. The Stackelberg Solution 102
Exercises 109

4. Typologies of Differential Games 111
4.1. Linear-Quadratic Games 114
4.1.1. Affine Equilibria 114
4.1.2. Stackelberg Solutions 121
4.2. Perfect Games 129
4.2.1. Trilinear, State-Redundant, and Exponential Games 129
4.2.2. Identifying Perfect Games 136
4.3. Qualitatively Solvable Games 139
4.3.1. Phase Diagram Analysis of Perfect Games 141
4.3.2. Symmetric Games with a Single State Variable 147
Exercises 150

5. Selected Applications 153
5.1. Faust—The Game 155
5.1.1. First Scenario—Goethe's Play 156
5.1.2. Second Scenario—The Original Source 160

5.2. The Dynamics of Oligopoly 162
5.2.1. The Finite Horizon Oligopoly 164
5.2.2. The Infinite Horizon Oligopoly 170
5.3. R & D Games 173
5.3.1. The Race for Priority 173
5.3.2. Market Structure and Research Intensity 178
5.4. Fishery Games 179
5.4.1. The Oligopolistic Fishery Game 179
5.4.2. Extinction, Conservation, and Economic Regulation 183
Exercises 186

References 189

Selected Bibliography 197

Index 201

1
Introduction

Everything has been thought of before, but the problem is to think of it again.

J.W. von Goethe

In this short chapter, we shall explain what is meant by differential games and sketch a history of this essential branch of game theory. Despite its convincing success in applied modeling, the discipline of differential games has gained a rather controversial reception in game theory circles. This is mainly due to the control-theory pronunciation of classical game theory vocables, apparently a violation of rules according to which some scientists play the game of game theory.

In the first part of the book, we will consequently prove that an accurate presentation of differential game concepts can be realized without neglecting basic game-theoretic rules of strategic interaction. The main emphasis, however, will be placed on the important features of dynamic informational play, which may be detected even after reduction of the differential game description to normal form. We shall furthermore illustrate how these dynamic properties may be translated into control-theoretic terms.

1.1. The Glass Bead Game

Hermann Hesse's "The Glass Bead Game" appeared in Switzerland in 1943. The conspicuous parallels between this literary fiction of "a game of thoughts called the Glass

Bead Game" and the theory of games,[1] born in 1944, can be taken as evidence that the times were ripe for the scientific and intellectual evolution of a discipline able to incorporate significant values of our culture.

Von Neumann and Morgenstern's[1] construct lacked the classical mathematical achievements in the spirit of Newton—a language of symbols in which science and art could play an equivalent role. It was Isaacs[2] who thought of such effective tools: differential equations. His optimal pursuit and evasion schemes represented a variation of an old theme, played once by Leonardo da Vinci.

The applications Isaacs had in mind were mainly combat problems. By its very nature the mathematics of (zero-sum) differential games seemed to restrict the Glass Bead Game to matters of martial arts.

1.1.1. Isaacs's Decade

The origins of differential game theory can be traced back to the late 1940s. Rufus Isaacs, then on appointment with Rand, formulated missile versus enemy aircraft pursuit schemes in terms of descriptive and navigation (state and control) variables, and found the main principle: the *tenet of transition.*

Further innovations in differential game techniques and basic concepts followed, but due to lack of financial support Isaacs's work did not appear in print until 1965. In the meantime the subject of control theory had reached its maturity; the *principle of optimality*—a one-player special case of the tenet of transition—had been put on the map.

Research in differential games seemed to concentrate

on the extension of control theory problems. Berkovitz[3] developed his variational approach to differential games; Leitmann and Mon[4] focused on geometric aspects of optimal control processes. Eastern games had started as well. Pontryagin[5] solved differential games by means of a maximum principle. Others were to follow.*

1.1.2. The Aftermath

The mathematicians made it a matter of principle to call Isaacs's basic results heuristic. Although they missed the point of his lesson, there was a great deal of room for improvement in rigorousness of mathematical formalization. Different approaches[7–9] have been proposed, e.g., to circumvent situations of incompatibility or indetermination—phenomena which are common to games utilizing feedback rules.

Isaacs's didactic procedure of expressing the most complex matters mainly by examples has been successfully used by Case[10,11] in his generalization of the Glass Bead Game to the nonzero-sum area of economic modeling. In treating this important class of differential games, it became obvious to draw heavily on classical game-theoretic results and concepts.

The analysis of intertemporal, nonantagonistic situations of conflict had a considerable impact on further progress in the area of differential games. These developments seem, however, to have escaped the traditional game theorists' attention. Even recent expositions[12,13] of

* A detailed account of differential game results in Soviet literature is given by Zaubermann.[6]

game theory contain, if any, an outdated and superficial account of differential game literature only.

We will try our best to close this informational gap by covering most of the conventional material of non-antagonistic differential game theory from an applied mathematical point of view. A good deal of attention will be devoted to the modeling of dynamic conflicting situations in operations research, management sciences, and economic theory. In this respect the contents of this book differ significantly from those of other books[14–18] on nonzero-sum differential games. The difference is both in the nature of exposition and in the choice of problems for which differential games may be applied.

1.2. Dynamic Models of Conflict

A salient feature of differential games is that they use the descriptive power of differential equations as a modeling tool. In this section (and throughout the book) we shall illustrate by (a handful of) different examples how differential games could in principle present an adequate way of explaining dynamic situations of conflict. A discerning reader will note that we do not cover the whole variety of possible applications. This (and subsequent) chapter(s) are not intended as a detailed catalog, but rather as the motivational foundation of the art of mathematical modeling through differential games.

1.2.1. A Compact with the Devil

The Faust legend is one of the most durable in Western folklore and literature. It is the story of a

German necromancer who sold his soul to the devil in exchange for knowledge and power. A great dramatic version of this legend has been created by Johann Wolfgang von Goethe. To motivate the use of differential game theory in the modeling of literary situations of conflict, we present now a brief epitome of Goethe's tragedy "Faust" in literary and mathematical terms (but only insofar as it affects our analysis). For a more accurate presentation see Mehlmann and Willing.[19]

The play's central theme is the compact between Faust and Mephisto. The conditions—which transform the compact into a wager—are clearly stated by the devil's promise:

> Then here below in service I'll abide
> Fulfilling tirelessly your last decree,

and by Faust's immortal words:

> If to the fleeting hour I say
> 'Remain, so fair thou art, remain'
> Then bind me with your fatal chain
> For I will perish in that day
> 'Tis I for whom the bell shall toll.
> Then you are free, your service done.
> For me the clock shall fail, to ruin run
> And timeless night descend upon my soul.

Translating these quotations* into mathematical terminology, we may define two probability distribution functions $x_i(\cdot)$ on $[0, \infty)$ that indicate the belief the ith player has about the timing of the "supreme Moment."

In Faust's view this moment can only be achieved by

* Reproduced by permission of Penguin Books Ltd.

striving activity. Having little faith in Mephisto's ability to achieve it by seduction, Faust is confident that he will win the bet—a melancholic prospect which means that he will never experience the magic instant. Denoting by $u_1(t)$ the seducing intensity and by $u_2(t)$ the striving intensity, we may thus assume that the hazard rate corresponding to $x_i(t)$ is a linear function of $u_i(t)$, that is,

$$\dot{x}_i = c_i u_i (1 - x_i), \qquad i = 1, 2 \tag{1.1}$$

where the c_i are positive constants.

Equation (1.1) describes the evolution in time of the state, x_i, $i = 1, 2$, in response to the control variables u_i. The initial state condition is given by

$$x_i(0) = 0, \qquad i = 1, 2 \tag{1.2}$$

There is, however, one additional ingredient missing: the criteria according to which the players strive to influence (by an adequate choice of their control variables) the state of the game over a finite interval of time, $[0, T]$. The expected payoff to Mephisto,

$$J_1 = \int_0^T [V\dot{x}_1 - (d_1 u_1^2 + d_2 u_2)(1 - x_1)]\, dt \tag{1.3}$$

consists of three terms—each weighted with the probability of the corresponding event. The devil will receive the amount V, the value of Faust's immortal soul, at instant t if the latter happens to be the critical moment. As long as this is not the case, seduction costs $d_1 u_1^2$ and Faust's striving activity gives birth to a disutility of $d_2 u_2$ units. The d_i are constant weights.

Faust does not pay attention to the loss of his soul. His payoff,

$$J_2 = \int_0^T [g_1 u_1(\bar{u} - u_1) + g_2 u_2(2u_1 - u_2)](1 - x_2)\, dt \qquad (1.4)$$

is influenced by the satisfaction derived from the devil's seduction and from the striving activity only. If $u_1(t)$ exceeds a given level $\bar{u}$ seduction will cause disutility. A negative effect on Faust's utility will also occur if the level of striving activity is larger than the present rate of seduction. The g_i are constant weights.

In our differential game formulation both $x_i(t)$ and $u_i(t)$ must be nonnegative. Thus, the (state independent) control constraints

$$0 \leqslant u_i < \infty, \qquad i = 1, 2 \qquad (1.5)$$

have to be imposed over $[0, T]$.

We shall return to this problem subsequently in illustrating solution concepts and methods of solution. The question we ultimately seek to answer is whether the above differential game provides a reasonable explanation of Faust's salvation as conceived by Goethe to terminate the play. This unusual game will be treated in Section 5.1.

1.2.2. A Game of Capitalism

Growth and distribution are the two fundamental determinants of what—in the Marxian view—might be called the essence of capitalism. Lancaster[20] posed the problem of wealth distribution between workers and capitalists in a Keynesian way. Its essentials are contained in the following differential game formulation:

$$\max_{c \leqslant u_1 \leqslant b} \left\{ J_1 = \int_0^T axu_1 \, dt \right\} \tag{1.6}$$

$$\max_{0 \leqslant u_2 \leqslant 1} \left\{ J_2 = \int_0^T ax(1-u_1)(1-u_2) \, dt + lx(T) \right\} \tag{1.7}$$

subject to

$$\dot{x} = ax(1-u_1)\,u_2; \qquad x(0) = x_0 \tag{1.8}$$

Workers try to maximize J_1—their consumption up to T—by controlling the ratio $u_1(t)$ of current worker's consumption to current output. According to condition (1.7), capitalists choose $u_2(t)$—the current proportion of remaining output to be invested—in such a way as to maximize both their own consumption over the same time horizon and a weighted evaluation of the final stock of capital.

The process of maximization pursued by either social group is constrained by control bounds and by equation (1.8), the dynamic equation for the growth of the capital stock $x(t)$. This equation characterizes the basic relationships of a simple economy, the technology of which is linear. The constant ratio of output to capital is denoted by a; the workers' control variable is bounded by

$$0 < c \leqslant u_1 \leqslant b < 1 \tag{1.9}$$

over $[0, T]$.

Note that Lancaster's paradigm of capitalism concentrates on the case $l < 1$, i.e., the capitalists take a lesser interest in posthorizon events than in those occurring within the horizon. The game and some of its variants will be analyzed in due course.

1.2.3. Strike Negotiation

Leitmann and Liu[21] proposed a model of negotiation between management and union during a strike. A simplified version of their game may be formulated as follows:

$$\min_{u_i} \left\{ J_i = \int_{t_0}^{t_f} a_i \, dt + (-1)^{(i-1)} x_i(t_f) \right\}, \quad i = 1, 2 \tag{1.10}$$

subject to

$$\dot{x}_i = (-1)^{(i-1)} u_i(x_2 - x_1); \qquad x_i(0) = x_{0i}, \qquad i = 1, 2 \tag{1.11}$$

$$x_{01} \leqslant x_1 \leqslant x_2 \leqslant x_{02} \tag{1.12}$$

and

$$t_f := \min\{t \geqslant 0 \mid x_2(t) - x_1(t) = m > 0\} \tag{1.13}$$

Management and union are bargaining over a certain issue, say, the total wages. The two sides may change the state of bargaining,

$$(x_1, x_2) = (\text{offer, demand}) \tag{1.14}$$

by concession rates $u_1(t)$ and $u_2(t)$, respectively. The positive constants a_i denote the instantaneous loss made by the ith player during a strike. Management chooses $0 \leqslant u_1(t) \leqslant \bar{u}_1$ so as to minimize the final offer and the total loss of profit during the process of bargaining. Union seeks to maximize the final demand and to minimize the total loss of wage over $[t_0, t_f]$ by an adequate choice of $0 \leqslant u_2(t) \leqslant \bar{u}_2$. The game terminates, when a certain state of bargaining is reached.

1.2.4. A Model of Duopolistic Competition

Simaan and Takayama[22] described the following dynamic duopoly game:

$$\max_{u_i \geqslant 0} \left\{ J_i = \int_0^T e^{-r_i t} [x u_i - c_i u_i - \tfrac{1}{2} \alpha_i u_i^2] \, dt \right\} \tag{1.15}$$

subject to

$$\dot{x} = k[a - b(u_1 + u_2) - x]; \qquad x(0) = x_0 \tag{1.16}$$

and

$$x(t) \geqslant 0 \qquad \text{for all} \quad t \in [0, T] \tag{1.17}$$

The players choose their output rate of production,

$$u_i(t) \geqslant 0 \tag{1.18}$$

so as to maximize J_i, the present value of the profit stream over $[0, T]$. Thereby, it is assumed that the change in price, $\dot{x}(t)$, is a function of the difference between the current market price, $x(t)$, and the price $\tilde{x}(t)$ determined by a linear demand function

$$\tilde{x}(t) = a - b[u_1(t) + u_2(t)]; \qquad a, b > 0 \qquad (1.19)$$

Each player has his own rate of time preference, r_i, and quadratic production costs.

An exhaustive analysis of this (differential) market competition game is given in Section 5.2.

1.2.5. The Competitive Limited-Access Fishery

A differential game approach to the study of the competitive limited-access fishery has been developed by Clark.[23] Each of N independent fishermen is faced with the decision at which rate of fishing effort,

$$0 \leqslant u_i(t) \leqslant \bar{u}_i \qquad (1.20)$$

to operate so as to maximize

$$\int_0^\infty e^{-r_i t} L_i(x, u_i)\, dt \qquad (1.21)$$

the total present value of his profit.

The size of the fish population at time t, $x(t)$, is given by solving the equation

$$\dot{x}(t) = G(x(t)) - \sum_{j=1}^{N} q_i u_i(t)\, x(t); \qquad x(0) = x_0 \qquad (1.22)$$

where q_i is the ith player's catchability coefficient; $G(\cdot)$ is a natural growth function satisfying

$$G(0) = G(\hat{x}) = 0; \qquad G(x) \geqslant 0 \qquad \text{for all} \quad 0 < x < \hat{x} \tag{1.23}$$

where $\hat{x}$ is the "carrying capacity."*

The ith player's instantaneous profit flow is assumed to satisfy

$$L_i(x, u_i) = (p_i q_i x - c_i)\, u_i \tag{1.24}$$

where c_i denotes the cost of effort and p_i the landed price of fish.

Fishery games will be discussed in Section 5.3.

1.3. Symbols and Terminology

1.3.1. Notation

The following symbols are adopted in the book:

$\in$	Is an element of
$\notin$	Is not an element of
$:=$	Defined by
$=$	Equality sign
$\neq$	Does not equal
$\approx$	Approximately equals
$\equiv$	Is identical to
$\gg$	Is much greater than
▮	End of proof, example, etc.

* The environmental saturation level.

$\subseteq$	Is a subset of
$\cup$	Union of sets
$\times, \prod$	Cartesian product
$\|\cdot\|$	Euclidean norm
$\lvert\cdot\rvert$	Absolute value
$'$	Transpose (of a vector, matrix)
$'$	First derivative (of a function)
$A-B$	Subtraction of sets; $A-B := \{c \mid c \in A, c \notin B\}$
a.e.	For all values except a set with measure zero
$\mathscr{A}_t(\phi_{-i})$	The ith player's attainable set of state values (at time t)
d.r.	Decision rule(s)
$\mathscr{D}$	Domain containing the playing space
$\mathscr{D}_k$, $k=1,\ldots, K$	Finite exhaustive decomposition of $\mathscr{D}$
$\mathscr{F}_i$	The ith player's set of Lipschitzean feedback rules
ϕ^*	Equilibrium of feedback rules
$g^i(t, u_i, x) \geqslant 0$	(State dependent) control constraints; g^i: $R \times R^{m_i} \times R^n \to R^{q_i}$
$\bar{g}(t, x) \geqslant 0$	State constraint(s); $\bar{g}$: $R \times R^n \to R^s$
$G_i(\cdot)$	C^2-diffeomorphism on X
ϕ^{tr}	Trigger strategy combination for Γ_T
$\mathscr{G}(\Xi)$	Transformed Hamiltonian game
$\Gamma_{[t,T]}$	Remaining subgame over $[t, T]$
$\gamma_i(x)$	Derivative of $G_i(\cdot)$ with respect to x
Γ_T	Finite horizon differential game
H_i	The ith player's Hamiltonian; $H_i(t, x, u, \mu_i) := L_i + \mu_i f$
$H_i^{\mathscr{G}}$	The ith player's transformed Hamiltonian

$\langle H_1,\ldots, H_N; U_1,\ldots, U_N\rangle$	Normal form of Ξ
$\langle {}^2H_1, {}^2H_2; U_1, U_1^{U_2}\rangle$	Normal form of ${}^2\Xi$
$\mathscr{I}_i(t)$	The ith player's information set at time t
inf	Infimum
J_i	The ith player's payoff
$\mathscr{J}_i$	Payoff corresponding to loop representation
$\langle \mathscr{J}_1,\ldots, \mathscr{J}_N; \mathscr{L}_1,\ldots, \mathscr{L}_N\rangle$	Normal form of Γ_T
l.d.r.	Loop decision rule(s)
lim	Limes
l_i	The ith player's l.d.r.
l_{-i}	$(N-1)$-tuple of actions (l.d.r.) $(l_1,\ldots, l_{i-1}, l_{i+1},\ldots, l_N)$
l^e	Equilibrium set of actions (l.d.r.)
l^t	Team optimal set of actions (l.d.r.)
$\lambda_i(\cdot)$	The ith player's costate (function)
Λ_i	The ith player's Lagrangean; $\Lambda_i := H_i + \bar{v}_i\bar{g} + v^ig^i$
$\mathscr{L}_i$	The ith player's set of l.d.r.
$\{\mathscr{L}_1,\ldots, \mathscr{L}_N\}$	Loop representation
max	Maximum
min	Minimum
$\mathscr{M}_{kl}$	Discontinuity manifolds
$\mu_i, \bar{v}_i, v_i$	The ith player's Hamiltonian and Lagrangean multipliers
N	Number of players
$\mathscr{O}$	Outcome set
$\Psi^2(u_1; t, x, \mu_2)$	The second player's best response set
Π_i	The ith player's security payoff level
R^n	n-Dimensional real space
sup	Supremum
$[t_0, T]$, $[t_0, \infty)$	Time intervals
u_i	The ith player's control variable

U_i	The ith player's control space; $U_i \subseteq R^{m_i}$
$u(\cdot)$	Outcome
$u_i(\cdot)$	The ith player's control path
$\mathscr{U}_i$	The ith player's set of control paths
$u^e(\cdot)$	Equilibrium outcome
$u^p(\cdot)$	Pareto-efficient outcome
$u^r(\cdot)$	Individually-rational outcome
$u^t(\cdot)$	Team optimal outcome
$u_t(\cdot)$	Outcome history over $[t_0, t)$
x	State variable
$\dot{x}(t)$	Time derivative of $x(t)$
$x(\cdot)$	State trajectory
X	State space; $X \subseteq R^n$
χ	Set of state trajectories
Ξ	Hamiltonian game
$^2\Xi$	Hamiltonian metagame (with reacting second player)

1.3.2. Related Terms

The following "glossary" contains definitions of mathematical and game-theoretic terms used (but not explicitly explained) in this book.

Absolute continuous function A member of the largest class of functions $f(\cdot)$ for which the indefinite *Lebesgue integral* $\int_a^x f'(t)\,dt$ equals $f(x) - f(a)$.

Bijective transformation A transformation $\mathscr{T}$ from a set $\mathscr{A}$ into a set $\mathscr{B}$ is called bijective if the set of all images $\mathscr{T}(a)$, $a \in \mathscr{A}$ is equal to $\mathscr{B}$ and if different points in $\mathscr{A}$ have different images.

Closure The set of all contact points of a given set.

Concave function A real-valued function $f(\cdot)$ is concave if the set of points below the graph of f is *convex*.

Constraint qualification A type of regularity condition imposed on the constraint functions in order to ensure the existence of (Lagrange) multipliers at the solution of a problem (of mathematical programming).

Convex set A set which contains for any two of its points, say, x and y, also the segment joining x and y.

Global asymptotic stability In terms of solutions to an autonomous system of differential equations, this property means that the (solution) paths converge toward a certain stationary point regardless of initial values.

Kuhn (game) tree A graphical representation based on the rules of play of a (finite alternative) game. Each node in the tree corresponds to a state of the game. Branches leading out of a node correspond to alternatives of action resulting from this state. A group of nodes may be joined to a certain player's information set. The other players are not allowed to distinguish among the members of this set.

Fundamental solution Any set of linearly independent solution vectors for the n-dimensional system of differential equations $\dot{y} = A(t)\,y$ (written in matrix form).

Lebesgue integral An integral of a function $f(\cdot)$ formed by grouping together points of the function's domain at which f takes neighboring values.

Local asymptotic stability In terms of solutions to an autonomous system of differential equations, this property means that the (solution) paths starting from initial values close to a certain stationary point converge toward this point.

Matrix-Riccati differential equation A differential equation which can be written in the form, say,

$$\dot{Z}(t) = Z(t)\,A(t)\,Z(t) + B(t)\,Z(t) + Z(t)\,C(t) + D(t)$$

where $A(t)$, $B(t)$, $C(t)$, $D(t)$ are matrices the elements of which are continuous functions of t on some time interval.

Maximum principle A general proposition reducing a dynamic optimization problem to an infinite set of static optimization problems each corresponding to an instant of the dynamic process.

Metagame A game which may be derived from a given N-person game in *normal form* by allowing a certain player (or even a certain group of players) to anticipate the other players' actions.

Negative definite A matrix A (and the associated quadratic form $z'Az$) is called negative definite if $z'Az$ is strictly negative for all values of z other than $z = 0$.

Negative semidefinite A matrix A (and the associated quadratic form $z'Az$) is called negative semidefinite if $z'Az$ is either negative or zero for all values of z other than $z = 0$.

Normal form game A game specified by a list $\langle \mathscr{P}_1, \ldots, \mathscr{P}_N; S_1, \ldots, S_N \rangle$ containing each player's action space S_i and payoff $\mathscr{P}_i$.

Piecewise continuous A function that has at most finitely many discontinuity points on, say, $[t_0, T]$, with one-sided limits at each such point.

Piecewise smooth A continuous function which admits a piecewise continuous first derivative.

Principle of optimality (Bellman's original formulation) "An optimal policy has the property that, whatever the initial state and initial decisions are, the remaining decisions constitute an optimal policy with regard to the state resulting from the first decision." (Compare the definition of a *sub-game perfect* equilibrium in Section 2.2.2.)

Rank of a matrix The number of linearly independent rows (or columns) in the matrix.

Repeated game A normal form game played more than once. The resulting game admits, of course, a new normal form presentation.

Structurally stable The behavior of solution paths to a structurally stable autonomous system of differential equations is not dramatically influenced by small perturbations in the system's equations.

Team problem A game in which the players' payoffs are identical (up to a scalar constant).

Tenet of transition (Isaacs's original formulation) "If the play proceeds from one position to a second and V (the *value of the game*) is thought of as known at the second, then it is determined at the first by demanding that the players optimize the increment of V during the transition." (Compare Theorem 2.4.)

Tragedy of the commons A paradigm for situations in which people are pursuing their own interests, although they could all benefit by cooperative action. (Hardin's original formulation: "Picture a pasture open to all. It is to be expected that each herdsman will try to keep as many cattle as possible on the commons... Therein is the tragedy. Each man is locked into a system that compels him to increase his herd without limit—in a world that is limited.")

Transition line A special (one-dimensional) discontinuity manifold crossed by the state trajectory corresponding to an equilibrium of feedback rules. It can arise only in differential games which are linear with respect to control variables. We refer the reader to Isaacs[2] and Başar and

Olsder[16] for a classification of singular surfaces in the context of zero-sum differential games.

Value of the game In a two-person, *zero-sum* game, the payoff that a player can ensure for himself irrespective of the other player's actions. (Compare the definition of *security payoff level* in Section 2.2.1.)

Zero-sum game A game in which the players' payoffs at every outcome sum to zero (or to a constant, in which case it can be easily converted to a zero-sum one).

2
Playing the Game

For when the one Great Scorer comes
To write against your name
He marks—not that you won or lost—
But how you played the game

Grantland Rice

In this chapter, we will introduce basic notions, concepts, and results which are required for understanding the essential ideas of differential game theory.

2.1. Rules of the Game

2.1.1. Basic Definitions

The preceding considerations of dynamic models of conflict may be summarized by arriving at the following mathematical description of a (*finite horizon*) differential game problem:

$$\max_{u_i \in U_i \subseteq R^{m_i}} \left\{ J_i = \int_{t_0}^{T} L_i(t, x, u_1, \ldots, u_N)\, dt + S_i(T, x(T)) \right\}, \quad i = 1, \ldots, N \qquad (2.1)$$

subject to

$$\dot{x} = f(t, x, u_1, \ldots, u_N); \qquad x(t_0) = x_0 \qquad (2.2)$$

$$x \in X \subseteq R^n \qquad (2.3)$$

Note that both the model of strike negotiation and the game of fishery do not fit in this framework.

Generalizations of the problem (2.1)–(2.3) to games which terminate under special conditions as well as to infinite horizon games will be treated in Chapter 3.

In a finite horizon game, Γ_T, N players act over a given (bounded) interval of time $[t_0, T]$ and within a system described by the (column) vector of *state variables*

$$x = (x_1, \ldots, x_n)' \tag{2.4}$$

The value of x is given at each instant t by a point in X, a subset of (n-dimensional real space) R^n.

The evolution of the state over time obeys the vector differential equation (2.2), where the vectors

$$u_i = (u_{i1}, \ldots, u_{im_i})' \tag{2.5}$$

of *control variables* are at the players' disposition, and x_0 denotes the system's *initial state*. The values of the u_i at time t are restricted to given subsets U_i of R^{m_i}.

Each player chooses a *control path* for his vector of control variables, that is, a piecewise continuous function $u_i(\cdot)$ on $[t_0, T]$ satisfying

$$u_i(t) \in U_i \tag{2.6}$$

for all $t \in [t_0, T]$. $\mathcal{U}_i$ will denote the ith player's set of control paths.

Definition 2.1. An N-tuple

$$u(\cdot) = (u_1(\cdot), \ldots, u_N(\cdot)) \tag{2.7}$$

is called an *outcome* of the game if there exists a continuous and piecewise smooth function $x(\cdot)$ on $[t_0, T]$ which is a unique solution to the initial value problem

$$\dot{x}(t) = f(t, x(t), u_1(t), ..., u_N(t)); \qquad x(t_0) = x_0 \quad (2.8)$$

and satisfies the state constraint

$$x(t) \in X \qquad \text{for all } t \in [t_0, T] \quad (2.9)$$

Function $x(\cdot)$ is called the *state trajectory* corresponding to the outcome $u(\cdot)$. The notations $\mathcal{O}$, $\mathcal{X}$ represent the game's outcome set and set of state trajectories, respectively.

Remark 2.1. Under circumstances which will be referred to in due course, we will have to admit Lebesgue integrable control functions satisfying the inclusion (2.6) almost everywhere (a.e.) on $[t_0, T]$. By a state trajectory corresponding to a Lebesgue integrable outcome we shall understand an absolutely continuous solution to (2.8).

With each outcome (and its corresponding state trajectory) we may associate the expressions

$$J_i(u_1(\cdot), ..., u_N(\cdot)) = \int_{t_0}^{T} L_i(t, x(t), u_1(t), ..., u_N(t))\, dt + S_i(T, x(T)) \quad (2.10)$$

for $i = 1, ..., N$.

We shall call $J_i(u_1(\cdot), ..., u_N(\cdot))$ the ith player's *payoff* corresponding to the outcome $u(\cdot)$ provided that the right-hand side of (2.10) is well defined.

For the time being we restrict consideration to those games (2.1)–(2.3) for which each selection of control paths leads to an outcome and to corresponding payoffs. This requires certain standard assumptions on the game's data; we shall postpone their statement to the examination of extensive and normal forms of play.

2.1.2. The Loop Model

The Kuhn model[24] for describing games in extensive form is based on the tree representation of a finite number of players' alternatives. In a differential game framework of uncountable many alternatives, it seems, however, that "only God can make a tree."* An alternative to the tree model, the *loop model*,[26,27] permits formulation of interaction between the moves of players in a differential game.

Let $\mathscr{L}_i$ denote a set of *loop decision rules* (l.d.r.)

$$l_i\colon \mathscr{O} \to \mathscr{U}_i \tag{2.11}$$

for the ith player. According to relation (2.11), each player chooses a control path on $[t_0, T]$ based on a sort of memory which does not necessarily work only backward. We shall, however, be interested mainly in nonanticipative rules that base any player's choice of control at time t on the game's outcome history over $[t_0, t)$ and, eventually, on additional information concerning current decisions taken by (one or more of) his contrahents.

* For an atheistic approach to tree genesis, see Mäkelä.[25]

A nonanticipative l.d.r. could be defined, e.g., by an induced mapping

$$l_i(u(\cdot))(t) := \sigma_i(t, x(t), u_1(t), \ldots, u_{i-1}(t), u_{i+1}(t), \ldots, u_N(t)) \tag{2.12}$$

where the function σ_i: $[t_0, T] \times X \times \prod_{j \neq i} U_j \to U_i$ is assumed to be piecewise continuous with respect to all arguments. The *induced* l.d.r. will be identified with σ_i, and will be called

$$\left\{\begin{array}{c}\text{an } \textit{open-loop} \\ \text{a } \textit{memoryless} \\ \text{a } (\textit{state}) \textit{ feedback}\end{array}\right\} \text{ decision rule,}$$

$$\text{if } \sigma_i \text{ is constant on } \left\{\begin{array}{c} X \times \prod_{j \neq i} U_j \\ X \\ \prod_{j \neq i} U_j \end{array}\right\}$$

Since we assume that the initial state x_0 [as well as the entire game structure (2.1)–(2.3)] is known *a priori* by all players, a possible dependence on (the constant) x_0 has not been made explicit in definition (2.12).

To be complete, a description of Γ_T must include:

1. The order in which the players' moves are prescribed to take place during each particular stage of an arbitrary, discrete time approximation of Γ_T.
2. Every player's instantaneous pattern of (access to) information which has become available after the beginning of play.

3. Whether preplay communication, binding agreements and other enforceable commitments about the players' future actions are possible.

The rules (1) and (2) specify the *situation of extensive play*; (3) indicates which type of *solutions theory* (cooperative or noncooperative) is likely to be adopted. Nonanticipative l.d.r. which are consistent with a given situation of extensive play will be called *strategies.*

Remark 2.2. In contrast to the Kuhn tree, where simultaneous play is modeled as if no (two) players move at the same point in time, an extensive loop formulation assumes that all players are making simultaneous choices at each instant t. Explicit knowledge of the players' actual order of moves is, however, revealed by (2).

Example 2.1. Consider the following induced l.d.r. for workers in Lancaster's game of capitalism (see Section 1.2.1)

$$u_1(t)=\begin{cases} b, & \text{if} \quad 1-\lambda_1(t)\,x(t)\,u_2(t)\geqslant 0 \\ c, & \text{otherwise} \end{cases} \tag{2.13}$$

Under the assumption that $\lambda_1(\cdot)$ is given in advance, the l.d.r. (2.13) is adapted to the following situation of extensive play: the capitalists move (or, equivalently, signalize their move) first, while the information available to the workers at each instant t is given by

$$\mathscr{I}_1(t)=\{x(t),\, u_2(t)\}$$

To adapt the workers' rule to a situation of simultaneous action, say,

$$\mathscr{I}_1(t) = \{x(t)\} = \mathscr{I}_2(t)$$

it would be necessary to have an *a priori* knowledge of the capitalists' control path, and to assume that their commitment to this path extends over the entire game horizon. Note that these two situations describe in fact different games. ∎

In the following we suppress any information concerning extensive play, and concentrate on the normal form description of Γ_T.

Definition 2.2. The game Γ_T is said to admit a *loop representation*

$$\{\mathscr{L}_1, \ldots, \mathscr{L}_N\}$$

if the simultaneous equations

$$l_i(u(\cdot)) = u_i(\cdot); \qquad i = 1, \ldots, N \tag{2.14}$$

are uniquely solvable on $\mathscr{O}$ for each selection

$$(l_1, \ldots, l_N); \qquad l_i \in \mathscr{L}_i, \qquad i = 1, \ldots, N \tag{2.15}$$

An admissible loop representation amounts essentially to reducing the differential game to an (equivalent) one-shot game, the *normal form* of Γ_T. The ith player's action in this game is simply the *a priori* choice of a l.d.r. $l_i \in \mathscr{L}_i$; payoffs may be defined by

$$\mathscr{J}_i(l_1, \dots, l_N) := J_i(u_1^*(\cdot), \dots, u_N^*(\cdot))$$

where the outcome $(u_1^*(\cdot), \dots, u_N^*(\cdot))$ denotes the unique solution of equation (2.14) corresponding to the N-tuple (2.15) of players' actions.

By treating l.d.r. as abstract objects, the normal form of a differential game neglects their actual meaning which may depend on rules of dynamic, strategic interaction. This actual loss of information provides, however, a reasonable resolution for paradoxical cases where, say, all players seem to react simultaneously each on his competitors' current decisions.

2.1.3. Generalized Concepts

We impose the following conditions on the game's data:

1. $X = R^n$.
2. The functions f and L_i, S_i, $i = 1, \dots, N$ are continuous and have continuous first partial derivatives with respect to state and control variables.
3. The partial derivatives of f with respect to state and control variables are uniformly bounded, that is, there exists a nonnegative constant K such that

$$\left\| \frac{\partial f(\diamond)}{\partial x} \right\| \leqslant K, \qquad \left\| \frac{\partial f(\diamond)}{\partial u_i} \right\| \leqslant K, \qquad i = 1, \dots, N$$

for all $(\diamond) = (t, x, u_1, \ldots, u_N) \in [t_0, T] \times R^n \times \prod_{j=1}^{N} U_j$, where $\| \quad \|$ refers to Euclidean norm in corresponding spaces.

Condition (1) certainly holds if the need to impose pure state constraints may be eliminated by satisfying reasonable control restrictions. See, for example, Faust's game where nonnegativity of control variables implies nonnegativity of state.

Theorem 2.1. Let the data of the differential game Γ_T satisfy the conditions (1)–(3), and denote by $\mathscr{F}_i$ the ith player's set of feedback decision rules which are defined by

$$l_i(u(\cdot))(t) := \phi_i(t, x(t))$$

and satisfy a (global) Lipschitz condition with respect to the state, that is, there exists a nonnegative constant, say, K_i, such that

$$\|\phi_i(t, x) - \phi_i(t, \tilde{x})\| \leqslant K_i \|x - \tilde{x}\|$$

for all $t \in [t_0, T]$, and $x, \tilde{x} \in R^n$. Then Γ_T admits a loop representation $\{\mathscr{F}_1, \ldots, \mathscr{F}_N\}$.

Proof. Under the assumptions stated above, each selection

$$(l_1, \ldots, l_N); \qquad l_i \in \mathscr{F}_i$$

leads to a unique, continuous and piecewise smooth solution $x_\phi(\cdot)$ to the initial value problem

$$\dot{x} = f(t, x, \phi_1(t, x), \ldots, \phi_N(t, x)); \qquad x(0) = x_0 \tag{2.16}$$

which is bounded on any bounded interval of time. Hence the outcome

$$(\phi_1[\cdot, x_\phi(\cdot)], \ldots, \phi_N[\cdot, x_\phi(\cdot)])$$

is a unique solution to the simultaneous equations

$$l_i(u(\cdot)) = u_i(\cdot); \qquad i = 1, \ldots, N$$

∎

The case of all players employing open-loop decision rules is implicit in the above. Since an open-loop d.r. may be identified with a control path, $\mathscr{U}_i$ will denote the ith player's set of open-loop decision rules.

An extension of the preceding results to more general types of l.d.r. is possible. It turns out that it suffices to consider, say, selections of induced l.d.r. (2.12) admitting a unique representation as elements of $\mathscr{F}_i$, $i = 1, \ldots, N$. For feedback rules which do not satisfy a (sort of) Lipschitz condition with respect to the state, the initial value problem (2.16) could have a solution but it may not be unique. Discontinuity in x could even make the problem intractable from a (classical) mathematical point of view.

To circumvent these difficulties, Friedman[(8)] and Krasovsky and Subbotin[(9)] proposed the approximation of discontinuous feedback rules by sequences of open-loop decision rules.

Let k_i, $i=1,\ldots, N$ denote positive integers. Define (for $i=1,\ldots, N$)

$$\Delta_i := (T-t_0)/k_i; \qquad t_j^{\Delta_i} := t_0 + j\Delta_i, \qquad j=0,\ldots, k_i$$

So given an N-tuple of feedback rules

$$l_i(u(\cdot))(t) = \phi_i(t, x(t)) \tag{2.17}$$

($i \in \{1,\ldots, N\}$), we may define for each selection k_i, $i=1,\ldots, N$, a corresponding N-tuple of open-loop rules

$$l_i^{\Delta_i}(u(\cdot))(t) = \phi_i(t, x^{\Delta}(t_{j-1}^{\Delta_i})) \qquad \text{for} \quad t \in [t_{j-1}^{\Delta_i}, t_j^{\Delta_i}) \tag{2.18}$$

where $j=1,\ldots, k_i$, $i=1,\ldots, N$, and $x^{\Delta}(\cdot)$ denotes the unique state trajectory emanating from x_0 and generated by rules (2.18), $i=1,\ldots, N$.

Under the additional assumptions:

4. For each $i \in \{1,\ldots, N\}$ the set U_i is compact (that is, a closed and bounded subset of Euclidean space).
5. The set $\{f(t, x, u_1,\ldots, u_N) \mid u_i \in U_i;\ i=1,\ldots, N\}$ is convex.

it may be shown that any sequence

$$\{x^{\Delta_m}(\cdot) \mid k_{i,m} \to \infty;\, i=1,\ldots, N \text{ for } m \to \infty\}$$

has a subsequence converging uniformly to some absolutely continuous state trajectory $x^*(\cdot)$. There exists, moreover, to each *generalized solution* $x^*(\cdot)$ a Lebesgue integrable outcome, say, $u^*(\cdot)$ such that

$$\dot{x}^*(t) = f(t, x^*(t), u^*(t))$$

holds a.e. on $[t_0, T]$.

Remark 2.3. Different subsequences may converge to different generalized solutions. A Lebesgue integrable outcome corresponding to a generalized solution may also not be unique. Under these circumstances, we shall propose a useful reduction of the players' payoffs to terms depending on the terminal state only. In fact, a payoff of type (2.1) can always be converted into one of terminal form by defining N additional state components

$$\dot{x}_{n+i} = L_i(t, x, u_1,..., u_N); \qquad x_{n+i}(t_0) = 0, \qquad i = 1,..., N$$

The conditions (1)–(4) remain unchanged. The function $f(\cdot)$ in (5) should be replaced by

$$\tilde{f}(\cdot) := \begin{pmatrix} f(\cdot) \\ L_1(\cdot) \\ \vdots \\ L_N(\cdot) \end{pmatrix}$$

Our prime interest is in weakening the curse of non-uniqueness. This is in fact quite easy to ensure by restricting consideration to those (non-Lipschitzean) feedback rules (2.17) for which all generalized solutions

$$(x_1^*(\cdot),..., x_{n+N}^*(\cdot))'$$

reach the same (terminal) payoff.

2.2. The Noncooperative Approach

The usual definition of a noncooperative solutions theory is one which neglects preplay communication and binding agreements. According to this definition, one might say that a noncooperative solutions theory is not able to discern games in which preplay communication and binding agreements are possible from those in which these devices are prohibited by rules. This blindness may, however, be removed by modeling cooperative rules as part of the formal context of the game. See, e.g., the differential game formulations of a binding agreement (Faust's compact with Mephisto) and a bargaining procedure (management versus union) which have been presented in Sections 1.2.1 and 1.2.3, respectively.

We shall adopt Harsanyi's[(28)] extension of the above definition where preplay communication is assumed for the purpose of coordination. A further effect of this extension, which is typical of infinitely repeated, one-shot games, but also of some classes of differential games, is that cooperative solutions may be sustained by means of noncooperative play.

2.2.1. Equilibria of (Normal Form) Actions

By making use of the normal form of Γ_T,

$$\langle \mathscr{I}_1, \ldots, \mathscr{I}_N; \mathscr{L}_1, \ldots, \mathscr{L}_N \rangle$$

a noncooperative solution of the game is given in terms of loop decision rules, selected according to some scheme of rational and stable behavior. A normal form solution will, certainly, have to satisfy additional (strategic) features in order to be consistent with extensive rules of play. Section 2.2.2 is primarily concerned with this problem.

Throughout this section we shall allow for an enlargement of the product space of normal form actions. We shall assume that there exists for each selection of the corresponding loop representation a maximal τ, $t_0 \leqslant \tau$, such that the simultaneous equations (2.14) are uniquely solvable on the outcome set of Γ_t, for all $t_0 \leqslant t < \tau$. Selections of normal form actions for which $\tau > T$ will be called *playable.*

It seems appropriate to start with a classification of outcomes.

Definition 2.3. An *i(ndividually)-rational* outcome, $u^{\mathrm{r}}(\cdot)$, is one which provides each player with at least his *security payoff level* Π_i, i.e.,

$$\Pi_i := \sup_{l_i} \inf_{l_{-i}} \mathscr{J}_i(l_1,\ldots, l_N) \leqslant J_i(u^{\mathrm{r}}(\cdot)) \qquad (2.19\text{a})$$

where l is playable, and l_{-i} denotes the $(N-1)$-tuple of actions $(l_1,\ldots, l_{i-1}, l_{i+1},\ldots, l_N)$. An outcome $u^{\mathrm{p}}(\cdot)$ is called *j(ointly)-rational* (*Pareto-efficient*), if there is no other outcome for which all players get a larger payoff, i.e.,

$$J_i(u(\cdot)) \geqslant J_i(u^{\mathrm{p}}(\cdot)) \qquad \text{for all } i$$
$$\Rightarrow J_i(u(\cdot)) = J_i(u^{\mathrm{p}}(\cdot)) \qquad \text{for all } i \qquad (2.19\text{b})$$

A Pareto-efficient outcome could be achieved by employing a *team optimal* set of actions, i.e., a playable N-tuple of l.d.r. l^{t} satisfying

$$\sum_{i=1}^{N} \alpha_i \mathscr{J}_i(l^{\mathrm{t}}) \geqslant \sum_{i=1}^{N} \alpha_i \mathscr{J}_i(l) \qquad (2.20)$$

for all $l \in \mathscr{L}_1 \times \cdots \times \mathscr{L}_N$ and a strictly positive constant $\alpha = (\alpha_1, \ldots, \alpha_N) \in R^N$, with $\sum_{i=1}^{N} \alpha_i = 1$.

An i-rational outcome could be achieved by employing an *equilibrium* set of actions, i.e., a playable N-tuple of l.d.r. l^{e} satisfying

$$\mathscr{J}_i(l^{\mathrm{e}}) \geqslant \mathscr{J}_i l_i \uparrow l^{\mathrm{e}}_{-i}) \tag{2.21}$$

for all $l_i \in \mathscr{L}_i$; $i = 1, \ldots, N$, such that

$$l_i \uparrow l^{\mathrm{e}}_{-i} := l^{\mathrm{e}}_1, \ldots, l^{\mathrm{e}}_{i-1}, l_i, l^{\mathrm{e}}_{i+1}, \ldots, l^{\mathrm{e}}_N$$

is playable.

By shifting from his equilibrium action, a selfish payoff-maximizing player will not gain under the assumption that the remaining players maintain their actions. This interpretation can, however, be justified only within an extensive (or repeated) game scenario.

Lemma 2.1. Any outcome $u^{\mathrm{e}}(\cdot)$ which uniquely corresponds to an equilibrium set of actions l^{e} is i-rational. Any outcome $u^{\mathrm{t}}(\cdot)$ which uniquely corresponds to a team optimal set of actions l^{t} is Pareto-efficient.

Proof. In view of (2.21) we have

$$J_i(u^{\mathrm{e}}(\cdot)) = \mathscr{J}_i(l^{\mathrm{e}}) \geqslant \mathscr{J}_i(l_i \uparrow l^{\mathrm{e}}_{-i}) \tag{2.22}$$

for all playable $l_i \uparrow l^{\mathrm{e}}_{-i}$, where $l_i \in \mathscr{L}_i$; $i = 1, \ldots, N$. From relation (2.22) we get

$$\mathscr{J}_i(l_i \uparrow l^{\mathrm{e}}_{-i}) \geqslant \inf_{l_{-i}} \mathscr{J}_i(l_i \uparrow l_{-i})$$

for all $l_i \in \mathscr{L}_i$; $i = 1,..., N$. Consequently we obtain

$$J_i(u^e(\cdot)) \geqslant \Pi_i \qquad \text{for all } i = 1,..., N$$

We leave it as an exercise for the reader to prove the second claim. ∎

Remark 2.4. To find a team optimal outcome, solve the control problem

$$\max_{u_1,...,u_N} \int_{t_0}^{T} \sum_{i=1}^{N} \alpha_i L_i(t, x, u_1,..., u_N)\, dt + S_i(T, x(T))$$

subject to

$$\dot{x} = f(t, x, u_1,..., u_N); \qquad x(t_0) = x_0$$

Note that each playable set of actions $\hat{l}$ generating this outcome is team optimal and an equilibrium of $\langle \sum_{i=1}^{N} \alpha_i \mathscr{J}_i,..., \sum_{i=1}^{N} \alpha_i \mathscr{J}_i; \mathscr{L}_1,..., \mathscr{L}_N \rangle$.

In what follows, we shall illustrate how equilibria of actions may be found. We are given the players' *Hamiltonians*

$$H_i(t, x, u, \mu_i) := L_i + \mu_i f, \qquad i = 1,..., N \tag{2.23}$$

where the row vector μ_i is a *multiplier* which may be identified (at each instant t) with a point in R^n.

Inspired by the technique of solving constrained (nonlinear) programming problems, we may seek at each instant t for an equilibrium of the N-player (normal form) *Hamiltonian game*

$$\Xi = \langle H_1, ..., H_N; U_1, ..., U_N \rangle$$

The ith player's action in this game is simply the choice of a point in U_i for the given values of $x, \mu_1, ..., \mu_N$; his payoff is given by H_i. Equilibria for this type of normal form game may be defined analogously to relation (2.21).

Example 2.2. Form the Hamiltonians

$$H_1 = (1 - x_1)[Vc_1 u_1 - d_1 u_1^2 - d_2 u_2] + \mu_{11} c_1 u_1 (1 - x_1) + \mu_{12} c_2 u_2 (1 - x_2) \tag{2.24a}$$

$$H_2 = (1 - x_2)[g_1 u_1 (\bar{u} - u_1) + g_2 u_2 (2u_1 - u_2)] + \mu_{21} c_1 u_1 (1 - x_1) + \mu_{22} c_2 u_2 (1 - x_2) \tag{2.24b}$$

for Faust's game. To avoid unnecessary details we neglect the control constraints (1.5), and exclude *a priori* the case $\{x_1 = 1\} \vee \{x_2 = 1\}$.

At each t the control value

$$u_2 = u_1 + \frac{\mu_{22} c_2}{2g_2} \tag{2.25}$$

is a maximum of function (2.24b) for the given values of $x_1 \neq 1$, $x_2 \neq 1$, u_1, μ_{21}, and μ_{22}. The relation (2.25) may be synthesized to either an open-loop or a memoryless decision rule. This choice will certainly influence the maximization of function (2.24a) with respect to u_1.

In the first case, the maximum of expression (2.24a) is given by

$$u_1^{\mathrm{a}} = \frac{c_1(V + \mu_{11})}{2d_1} \tag{2.26a}$$

In the second case, Mephisto's (the first player's) maximizing control may be derived by keeping Faust's reaction on the choice of u_1 in mind, i.e.,

$$u_1^{\mathrm{b}} = \frac{c_1(V + \mu_{11}) - d_2 + c_2\mu_{12}(1 - x_2)(1 - x_1)^{-1}}{2d_1} \tag{2.26b}$$

This situation is, unfortunately, not consistent with the normal form representation of the Hamiltonian game. It would, however, perfectly fit the following Hamiltonian *metagame**

$$^2\Xi = \langle {}^2H_1, {}^2H_2; U_1, U_1^{U_2} \rangle \tag{2.27}$$

where Faust's (the second player's) space of (re)actions $U_1^{U_2}$ is the set of mappings ρ_2 from U_1 into U_2 and

$$^2H_i(\ldots, u_1, \rho_2, \ldots) := H_i(\ldots, u_1, \rho_2(u_1), \ldots) \tag{2.28}$$

for $i = 1, 2$. Note that metagames can be used to retain explicit knowledge of the players' extensive move structure.

* For a detailed exposition of metagame theory, see Howard.[29]

In the light of the results obtained,

$$(u_1^a, \rho_2^a); \qquad \rho_2^a(u_1) = u_1^a + \frac{\mu_{22} c_2}{2g_2} \tag{2.29a}$$

$$(u_1^b, \rho_2^b); \qquad \rho_2^b(u_1) = u_1^b + \frac{\mu_{22} c_2}{2g_2} \tag{2.29b}$$

are equilibria of the Hamiltonian metagame ${}^2\Xi$.

Since the constant reaction ρ_2^a may be identified with the control value

$$u_1^a + \frac{\mu_{22} c_2}{2g_2}$$

expression (2.29a) is a (unique) equilibrium of the Hamiltonian game Ξ as well. ∎

In order to facilitate present exposition, suppose that we are given an equilibrium of feedback rules ϕ^*, defined by

$$\phi^*(t, x) = (\phi_1^*(t, x), ..., \phi_N^*(t, x)) \tag{2.30}$$

where each $\phi_i^*(t, x)$, $i = 1, ..., N$ is a continuously differentiable function of x. At discontinuity points $\tau \in \Delta$ [where Δ is a finite subset of (t_0, T)] each $\phi_i^*(t, x)$ is assumed to be right (or left) continuous. Note that condition (2) (as stated in Section 2.1.3) remains in force.

Theorem 2.2. Let $x^*(\cdot)$ denote the unique state trajectory corresponding to relation (2.30). Then the outcome value $\phi^*(t, x^*(t))$ is at each $t \in [t_0, T] - \Delta$ an equilibrium of Ξ for $x = x^*(t)$ and $\mu_i = \lambda_i(t)$, $i = 1,\ldots, N$, with the continuous and piecewise continuously differentiable functions $\lambda_i(\cdot)$ satisfying

$$\dot{\lambda}_i(t) = -\frac{\partial H_i^*}{\partial x} - \sum_{j \neq i} \frac{\partial H_i^*}{\partial u_j} \frac{\partial \phi_j^*(t, x^*(t))}{\partial x} \tag{2.31a}$$

$$\lambda_i(T) = \frac{\partial S_i(T, x^*(T))}{\partial x} \tag{2.31b}$$

on $[t_0, T] - \Delta$. (By $\partial H_i^*/\partial \cdot$ we understand the term $\partial H_i/\partial \cdot$ evaluated at t, $x = x^*(t)$, $u = \phi^*(t, x^*(t))$, and $\mu_i = \lambda_i(t)$.)

Proof. If we are given an equilibrium of feedback rules (2.30), then, by definition (2.21), each control path $\phi_i^*(\cdot, x^*(\cdot))$, $i = 1,\ldots, N$, is an optimal solution to the control problem

$$\max_{u_i} \int_{t_0}^{T} L_i[t, x, u_i \uparrow \phi_{-i}^*(t, x)]\, dt + S_i(T, x(T))$$

subject to

$$\dot{x} = f[t, x, u_i \uparrow \phi_{-i}^*(t, x)]; \qquad x(t_0) = x_0$$

The result stated above follows immediately from the *maximum principle** of optimal control theory. ∎

* Pontryagin's famous result can, for instance, be found in Kamien and Schwartz,[30] Sethi and Thompson,[31] Feichtinger and Hartl,[32] and Seierstad and Sydsæter.[33]

Starting from an equilibrium of Ξ, say,

$$\hat{u}^*(t, x, \mu_1, \ldots, \mu_N) = (\hat{u}_1^*(t, x, \mu_1, \ldots, \mu_N), \ldots, \hat{u}_N^*(t, x, \mu_1, \ldots, \mu_N)) \tag{2.32}$$

candidates ϕ^* for an equilibrium of feedback rules may be derived by solving the set of differential equations (2.31a,b), $i = 1, \ldots, N$, under the additional restriction

$$\phi^*(t, x^*(t)) = \hat{u}^*(t, x^*(t), \lambda_1(t), \ldots, \lambda_N(t)) \tag{2.33}$$

for all $t \in [t_0, T]$, and with $x^*(\cdot)$ given by

$$\dot{x}^* = f[t, x^*, \phi^*(t, x^*(t))]; \qquad x^*(t_0) = x_0$$

Example 2.3. Recall Lancaster's game of capitalism. Suppose that $l = 0$ and $x_0 > 0$. The pair of control values

$$\hat{u}_1^*(\mu_1, \mu_2) = \begin{cases} b & \text{if} \quad 1 - \mu_1 \hat{u}_2^*(\mu_2) > 0 \\ d_1 & \text{if} \quad 1 - \mu_1 \hat{u}_2^*(\mu_2) = 0 \\ c & \text{otherwise} \end{cases} \tag{2.34a}$$

and

$$\hat{u}_2^*(\mu_2) = \begin{cases} 1 & \text{if} \quad \mu_2 - 1 > 0 \\ d_2 & \text{if} \quad \mu_2 - 1 = 0 \\ 0 & \text{otherwise} \end{cases} \tag{2.34b}$$

is at each t [and for arbitrary $(d_1, d_2) \in [c, b] \times [0, 1]$] an equilibrium of the corresponding Hamiltonian game.

We seek to solve the following set of equations:

$$\dot{\lambda}_1(t) = -a\phi_1^*(t, x^*(t)) - \lambda_1(t)\, a[1 - \phi_1^*(t, x^*(t))] \times \left[\phi_2^*(t, x^*(t)) + x^*(t)\frac{\partial \phi_2^*(t, x^*(t))}{\partial x}\right];$$

$$\lambda_1(T) = 0 \tag{2.35a}$$

$$\dot{\lambda}_2(t) = \{-a[1 - \phi_2^*(t, x^*(t))] - \lambda_2(t)\, a\phi_2^*(t, x^*(t))\} \times \left\{[1 - \phi_1^*(t, x^*(t))] - x^*(t)\frac{\partial \phi_1(t, x^*(t))}{\partial x}\right\};$$

$$\lambda_2(T) = l = 0 \tag{2.35b}$$

$$\dot{x}^*(t) = ax^*(t)[1 - \phi_1^*(t, x^*(t))]\, \phi_2^*(t, x^*(t)); \qquad x^*(0) = x_0 \tag{2.35c}$$

with the unknown functions ϕ_i^*, $i = 1, 2$, satisfying

$$\phi_1^*(t, x^*(t)) = \hat{u}_1^*(\lambda_1(t), \lambda_2(t)) \tag{2.36a}$$

$$\phi_2^*(t, x^*(t)) = \hat{u}_2^*(\lambda_2(t)) \tag{2.36b}$$

for all $t \in [0, T]$.

Since the expressions (2.34a,b) do not depend on x, we can initially just consider open-loop decision rules, i.e., piecewise and right continuous functions $\phi_i^*(\cdot)$, $i = 1, 2$, given at each instant t by the right-hand sides of conditions (2.36a,b). Under these assumptions, the functions $\lambda_i(\cdot)$, $i = 1, 2$, are strictly decreasing on $[0, T]$. In consequence, it follows from $\lambda_2(T) = 0$ and (2.34a,b) that

$$\phi_1^*(t) = b; \qquad \phi_2^*(t) = 0 \tag{2.37}$$

for all $t \in [0, T]$ such that $\lambda_2(t) < 1$. Solving equations (2.35a,b) for the values given by relations (2.37), we obtain

$$\lambda_1(t) = ab(T-t); \qquad \lambda_2(t) = a(1-b)(T-t) \tag{2.38}$$

Hence $\bar{t} = T - 1/[a(1-b)]$ is the instant at which $\lambda_2(t)$ equals 1.

For $\bar{t} > 0$ and $b > 1/2$ it is readily verified that the pair of open-loop decision rules

$$\phi_1^*(t) = \begin{cases} b & \text{if } \quad t \geqslant \bar{t} \\ c & \text{otherwise} \end{cases} \tag{2.39a}$$

and

$$\phi_2^*(t) = \begin{cases} 0 & \text{if } \quad t \geqslant \bar{t} \\ 1 & \text{otherwise} \end{cases} \tag{2.39b}$$

satisfies the necessary conditions stated in Theorem 2.2. ▮

In the remainder of this section, conditions for sufficiently smooth N-tuples of feedback rules to be equilibria are presented. Let $X \subseteq R^n$ denote an open, convex subset of state space to which the values of state trajectories imposed by the control restrictions U_i, $i = 1,\ldots, N$, necessarily belong.

Let $y_i = G_i(x)$, $i = 1,\ldots, N$, define a selection of (not necessarily different) C^2-diffeomorphisms on X, i.e., functions G_i, (at least) twice continuously differentiable on X, that have (each) an (at least) twice continuously differentiable inverse G_i^{-1} on, say, convex sets $Y_i = G_i(X) \subseteq R^n$. Denote by $\gamma_i(x)$ the derivative of G_i with respect to x, and by $\mathscr{G}(\Xi)$ the *transformed* Hamiltonian game

$$\mathscr{G}(\Xi) = \langle H_1^{\mathscr{G}},..., H_N^{\mathscr{G}}; U_1,..., U_N \rangle$$

where the (transformed) Hamiltonians $H_i^{\mathscr{G}}$, $i = 1,..., N$, are given by

$$H_i^{\mathscr{G}}(t, y_i, u, v_i) := H_i[t, G_i^{-1}(y_i), u, v_i \gamma_i(G_i^{-1}(y_i))] \quad (2.40)$$

with multipliers v_i.

Theorem 2.3. Suppose that

$$\phi^*(t, x) := \hat{u}^*(t, x, \eta_1(t)\,\gamma_1(x),..., \eta_N \gamma_N(x)) \quad (2.41)$$

defines a sufficiently smooth N-tuple of feedback rules, ϕ^*, with corresponding unique state trajectory $x^*(\cdot)$, and that the functions $\lambda_i(\cdot) = \eta_i(\cdot)\,\gamma_i(x^*(\cdot))$, $i = 1,..., N$, satisfy equations (2.31a,b) on $[t_0, T]$. If the functions

$$S_i[T, G_i^{-1}(y_i(T))]$$

and

$$H_i[t, y_i, \phi^*(t, G_i^{-1}(y_i)), \eta_i(t)], \qquad i = 1,..., N$$

are concave with respect to $y_i \in Y_i$ (at each instant $t \in [t_0, T]$), then ϕ^* is an equilibrium.

Proof. In view of relation (2.41), the N-tuple of control values $\phi^*(t, G_i^{-1}(y_i))$ is at each $(t, y_i) \in [t_0, T] \times Y_i$

an equilibrium of $\mathscr{G}(\Xi)$ for $v_i = \eta_i(t)$. Consequently, we have

$$H_i^{\mathscr{G}}[t, y_i, \phi^*(t, G_i^{-1}(y_i)), \eta_i(t)] \geqslant H_i^{\mathscr{G}}[t, y_i, u_i \uparrow \phi^*_{-i}(t, G_i^{-1}(y_i)), \eta_i(t)] \quad (2.42)$$

for all $u_i \in U_i$, $i = 1,..., N$.

From concavity of $H_i^{\mathscr{G}}[t, y_i, \phi^*(t, G_i^{-1}(y_i)), \eta_i(t)]$ with respect to y_i we derive

$$H_i^{\mathscr{G}}[t, \hat{y}_i, \phi^*(t, G_i^{-1}(\hat{y}_i)), \eta_i(t)] - H_i^{\mathscr{G}}[t, \bar{y}_i, \phi^*(t, G_i^{-1}(\bar{y}_i)), \eta_i(t)] \geqslant \left\{\frac{d}{dy} H_i^{\mathscr{G}}[t, \hat{y}_i, \phi^*(t, G_i^{-1}(\hat{y}_i)), \eta_i(t)]\right\} (\hat{y}_i - \bar{y}_i) \quad (2.43)$$

for all $\hat{y}_i, \bar{y}_i \in Y_i$. We must show that

$$\mathscr{J}_i(\phi^*) - \mathscr{J}_i(\phi_i \uparrow \phi^*_{-i}) \geqslant 0 \quad (2.44)$$

for all playable $\phi_i \uparrow \phi^*_{-i}$, $i = 1,..., N$. Let $\tilde{x}(\cdot)$ denote the unique state trajectory corresponding to the N-tuple of feedback rules $\phi_i \uparrow \phi^*_{-i}$. Define

$$y_i^*(\cdot) := G_i(x^*(\cdot)); \qquad \tilde{y}_i(\cdot) := G_i(\tilde{x}(\cdot)) \quad (2.45)$$

Then, we have

$$
\begin{aligned}
&\mathscr{J}_i(\phi^*) - \mathscr{J}_i(\phi_i \uparrow \phi^*_{-i}) \\
&\quad = \int_{t_0}^{T} \{L_i[t, x^*(t), \phi^*(t, x^*(t))] \\
&\qquad\qquad - L_i[t, \tilde{x}(t), \phi_i(t, \tilde{x}(t)) \uparrow \phi^*_{-i}(t, \tilde{x}(t))]\}\, dt \\
&\qquad + S_i(T, x^*(T)) - S_i(T, \tilde{x}(T)) \\
&\quad = \int_{t_0}^{T} \{L_i[t, G_i^{-1}(y_i^*(t)), \phi^*[t, G_i^{-1}(y_i^*(t))]] \\
&\qquad\qquad - L_i[t, G_i^{-1}(\tilde{y}_i(t)), \phi_i[t, G_i^{-1}(\tilde{y}_i(t))] \\
&\qquad\qquad \uparrow \phi^*_{-i}[t, G_i^{-1}(\tilde{y}_i(t))]]\}\, dt \\
&\qquad + S_i[T, G_i^{-1}(y_i^*(T))] - S_i[T, G_i^{-1}(\tilde{y}_i(T))]
\end{aligned} \tag{2.46}
$$

From relations (2.42) and (2.43) and concavity of $S_i[T, G_i^{-1}(y_i(T))]$ with respect to y_i, there follows

$$
\begin{aligned}
&\mathscr{J}_i(\phi^*) - \mathscr{J}_i(\phi_i \uparrow \phi^*_{-i}) \\
&\quad \geqslant \int_{t_0}^{T} \left\{ \left\{ \frac{d}{y_i} H_i^{\mathscr{G}}[t, y_i^*(t), \phi^*[t, G_i^{-1}(y_i^*(t))], \eta_i(t)] \right\} \right. \\
&\qquad\qquad \times (y_i^*(t) - \tilde{y}_i(t)) \\
&\qquad\qquad \left. - \eta_i(t)(\dot{y}_i^*(t) - \dot{\tilde{y}}_i(t)) \right\} dt \\
&\qquad + \left\{ \frac{\partial}{\partial y_i} S_i[T, G_i^{-1}(y_i^*(T))] \right\} (y_i^*(T) - \tilde{y}_i(T))
\end{aligned} \tag{2.47}
$$

Since $\lambda_i(\cdot)=\eta_i(\cdot)\,\gamma_i(x^*(\cdot))$ satisfies equations (2.31a,b) on $[t_0, T]$, we have

$$\dot{\eta}_i(t) = -\frac{\partial(H_i^{\mathscr{G}})^*}{\partial y_i} - \sum_{j\neq i} \frac{\partial(H_i^{\mathscr{G}})^*}{\partial u_j}\frac{\partial}{\partial y_i}\phi_j^*[t, G_i^{-1}(y_i^*(t))] \tag{2.48a}$$

$$\eta_i(T) = \frac{\partial}{\partial y_i} S_i[T, G_i^{-1}(y_i^*(T))] \tag{2.48b}$$

where $\partial(H_i^{\mathscr{G}})^*/\partial\cdot$ denotes the evaluation of $\partial H_i^{\mathscr{G}}/\partial\cdot$ at

$t, \quad y_i = y_i^*(t), \quad u=\phi^*[t, G_i^{-1}(y_i^*(t))], \quad$ and $\quad v_i = \eta_i(t)$

But the right-hand side of equation (2.48a) equals

$$\frac{d}{dy_i} H_i^{\mathscr{G}}[t, y_i^*(t), \phi^*[t, G_i^{-1}(y_i^*(t))], \eta_i(t)]$$

as may be shown by invoking the so-called *envelope theorem.** Therefore

$$\begin{aligned}
&\mathscr{J}_i(\phi^*) - \mathscr{J}_i(\phi_i \uparrow \phi_{-i}^*) \\
&\qquad \geqslant \int_{t_0}^{T} [-\dot{\eta}_i(t)(y_i^*(t) - \tilde{y}_i(t)) - \eta_i(t)(\dot{y}_i^*(t) - \dot{\tilde{y}}_i(t))]\, dt \\
&\qquad\quad + \eta_i(T)(y_i^*(T) - \tilde{y}_i(T)) \\
&\qquad = \eta_i(T)(y_i^*(t_0) - \tilde{y}_i(t_0))
\end{aligned} \tag{2.49}$$

The equality $y_i^*(t_0) = \tilde{y}_i(t_0) = y_i(x_0)$ completes the proof. ∎

In view of Theorem 2.3, the pair of open-loop

* See Feichtinger and Hartl.[32]

decision rules (2.39a,b) qualifies as an equilibrium. (To see this, take $y_i = x$ for all $i = 1,..., N$.)

2.2.2. Strategic Features

Let l^e be an equilibrium of normal form actions which is adaptable to a given situation of extensive play, and denote by $u^e(\cdot)$ the corresponding unique outcome. By allowing communication for the purpose of coordination, players can agree to stabilize this outcome against individual violation of the *status quo* by changing strategies in the course of play. An enforcement of this agreement has to be guaranteed by a silent threat players never explicitly announce: to stick to their equilibrium strategies. (Even though there may exist other strategies yielding the same payoff. See Harsanyi[34] for a discussion of the enforcement problem. According to his terminology, we are in the realm of an "almost-noncooperative" games theory.)

A threat is called *efficient* if neither player gains anything by violating the *status quo* in the course of play; it will be called *credible* if the punitive action would be in the interest of the threatening side, each time the threat has to be carried out.

Under the assumption of extensive play, the game Γ_T might be seen as consisting (at each intermediate time $t_0 < t < T$) of the outcome history $u_t(\cdot)$ over $[t_0, t)$ and the remaining subgame $\Gamma_{[t,T]}$. The latter starts at time t and at the new initial state

$$x(t) = \int_{t_0}^{t-0} f(\tau, x(\tau), u_t(\tau))\, d\tau + x_0$$

and is played according to the same rules as Γ_T.

Definition 2.4. l^e is called a *time consistent* equilibrium of Γ_T, if it induces an equilibrium on $\Gamma_{[t,T]}$ for all $t \in (t_0, T)$ and all $u_t(\cdot) = u_t^e(\cdot)$. l^e is called a *subgame perfect* equilibrium of Γ_T, if it induces an equilibrium on $\Gamma_{[t,T]}$ for all $t \in (t_0, T)$ and all possible $u_t(\cdot)$.

Whereas in Kuhn trees there may exist subgame perfect equilibria that prescribe noncredible behavior at certain information sets, the informational transcription of Selten's[(35)] *subgame perfectness* to an extensive (nonanticipative) loop formulation (see Remark 2.2) generates only credible and efficient (silent) threats.

For the present we consider feedback equilibria adapted to the extensive situation of simultaneous action

$$\mathscr{I}_i(t) = \{x(t)\}; \qquad i = 1, \ldots, N \tag{2.50}$$

The following theorem provides a tool of obtaining subgame perfect equilibria by solving partial differential equations, which are related to the (Hamilton–Jacobi–) Bellman equation of dynamic programming.

Theorem 2.4. Suppose that V_i, $i = 1, \ldots, N$, are smooth functions defined on $[t_0, T] \times X$, and that each V_i satisfies the partial differential equation

$$-\frac{\partial}{\partial t} V_i(t, x) = H_i\left(t, x, \hat{\phi}(t, x), \frac{\partial}{\partial x} V_i(t, x)\right) \tag{2.51a}$$

$$V_i(T, x) = S_i(T, x) \tag{2.51b}$$

where the N-tuple $\hat{\phi}$ of feedback strategies is given by

$$\hat{\phi}(t, x) := \hat{u}^* \left(t, x, \frac{\partial}{\partial x} V_1(t, x), \ldots, \frac{\partial}{\partial x} V_N(t, x) \right) \tag{2.52}$$

If the N-tuple of feedback strategies induced on the subgame $\Gamma_{[\tau, T]]}$, $x(\tau) = \xi$, by $\hat{\phi}$ is playable at each $(\tau, \xi) \in (t_0, T) \times X$, then $\hat{\phi}$ is a subgame perfect equilibrium.

Proof. From relations (2.52) and (2.51a) we derive

$$\begin{aligned} 0 &= L_i[t, \hat{x}(t), \hat{\phi}(t, \hat{x}(t))] + \frac{d}{dt} V_i(t, \hat{x}(t)) \\ &\geqslant L_i[t, x^i(t), \phi_i(t, x^i(T)) \uparrow \hat{\phi}_i(t, x^i(t)] + \frac{d}{dt} V_i(t, x^i(t)) \end{aligned} \tag{2.53}$$

for all $i = 1, \ldots, N$ and all $t \in [\tau, T]$, $\tau \geqslant t_0$, where $\hat{x}(\cdot)$ and $x^i(\cdot)$ are the unique state trajectories generated by playable N-tuples of feedback strategies induced on the subgame $\Gamma_{[\tau, T]}$, $x(\tau) = \xi$, by $\hat{\phi}$ and $\phi_i \uparrow \hat{\phi}_{-i}$.

Integrating equation (2.53) from τ to T, we obtain

$$\begin{aligned} V_i(\tau, \xi) &= \int_\tau^T L_i[t, \hat{x}(t), \hat{\phi}(t, \hat{x}(t))] \, dt + S_i(T, \hat{x}(T)) \\ &\geqslant \int_\tau^T L_i[t, x^i(t), \phi_i \uparrow \hat{\phi}_{-i}(t, x^i(t))] \, dt \\ &\quad + S_i(T, x^i(T)) \end{aligned} \tag{2.54}$$

for all $i = 1, \ldots, N$; $(\tau, \xi) \in [t_0, T] \times X$ and all admissible ϕ_i.

From relation (2.54) it readily follows that function (2.52) is a subgame perfect equilibrium of Γ_T. ∎

Feedback equilibria found by means of relation (2.41) may tacitly depend on the equilibrium state trajectory and, consequently, on the initial state x_0. This is due to the fact that relations (2.48a,b) are often equations involving $x^*(\cdot)$. Note that these equilibria are time consistent but, in general, not subgame perfect. [An exception to this rule is given by the equilibrium (2.39a,b).]

If we restrict consideration to induced loop decision rules, the normal form of Γ_T does provide enough structure to differentiate (sufficiently smooth) subgame perfect equilibria from the others. This is due to the fact that, under these circumstances, subgame perfectness may be considered as equivalent to robustness against perturbations in the initial state value. This result follows easily from the relationship between dynamic programming and the maximum principle (Fleming and Rishel,[36] Chapter iv).

Subgame imperfect equilibria are credible under precommitment only. A subgame perfect equilibrium may, however, be used as a punishment mode when players agree to play a certain outcome whose associated payoffs are higher (for every player) than are the equilibrium payoffs.

Assume that the players' payoffs in Γ_T have been converted to terms depending on the terminal state only, i.e., the (new) vector of state variables has two components $x^1 \in R^n$, $x^2 \in R^n$, the last of which will correspond to the N additional state variables (see Remark 2.3). We shall proceed under the conditions (1)–(5) stated in Section 2.1.3. Let $\hat{\phi}$ be a subgame perfect, feedback equilibrium, and denote by $\hat{x}[\cdot; \tau, \xi]$ the corresponding unique state trajectory starting at $x^1(\tau) = \xi$; $x^2(\tau) = 0$. Let $\tilde{u}(\cdot)$ be an outcome, and denote by $\tilde{x}(\cdot)$ the corresponding unique state trajectory starting at $x^1(t_0) = x_0$; $x^2(t_0) = 0$.

We shall consider a new state y having components

$$y = \begin{pmatrix} y_1 \\ y_2 \\ y_3 \end{pmatrix}; \qquad y^i = x^i - \tilde{x}^i, \qquad i = 1, 2;$$

$$\dot{y}^3 = (x - \tilde{x})^2, \qquad y^3(t_0) = 0 \tag{2.55}$$

Define an N-tuple ϕ^{tr} of discontinuous feedback rules by

$$\phi_i^{\text{tr}}(t, y) = \begin{cases} \tilde{u}_i(t), & \text{if } \ y = 0 \\ \hat{\phi}_i(t, y^1 + \tilde{x}^1), & \text{otherwise} \end{cases} \qquad i = 1, \ldots, N \tag{2.56}$$

ϕ^{tr} is called a *trigger strategy combination* for Γ_T, if the information assumed to be available to each player at time t implies that he knows $y(t)$ as well. Using this knowledge, each player can observe the consequences of the other players' behavior.

According to equation (2.56), the ith player's strategy is to obey the agreement to play $\tilde{u}(\cdot)$ as long as the others (apparently) do, but to switch to his subgame perfect equilibrium strategy if someone deviates from the expected pattern of behavior. Note that the component y^3 permits the players to recall the possible (individual) deviation from the agreement in the past.

Remark 2.5. The use of a new "history-dependent"

state variable illustrates the point that in differential games there is absolutely no need to base dynamic behavior on an infinite amount of information. Characterizations of trigger strategy combinations in repeated (one-shot) games have been provided by Radner[(37)] and Friedman.[(13)] For a first treatment in the context of differential games, see Tołwinski *et al.*[(38)] The following theorem and its proof are essentially theirs.* Ours is the use of a "history-dependent" state variable in a (state-) feedback context, a necessary generalization of Fershtman.[(39)]

Theorem 2.5. Let ϕ^{tr} be a trigger strategy combination for Γ_T. If

$$S_i(T, \hat{x}^1[T; \tau, \tilde{x}^1(\tau)]) + \hat{x}_i^2[T; \tau, \tilde{x}^1(\tau)] \leqslant S_i(T, \tilde{x}^1(T)) + \tilde{x}_i^2(T) \tag{2.57}$$

for all $\tau \in [t_0, T)$ and all $i = 1,..., N$, then ϕ^{tr} is a subgame perfect equilibrium of Γ_T.

Proof. In proving the theorem, we keep in mind that discontinuous feedback strategies have to be approximated by sequences of open-loop decision rules (see Section 2.1.3). Note that ϕ^{tr} generates $\tilde{x}(\cdot)$ as corresponding unique state trajectory. Consider an N-tuple of feedback strategies $\phi_i \uparrow \phi^{\text{tr}}_{-i}$ with ϕ_i being an arbitrary (possibly discontinuous) strategy for the ith player. Let $x^*(\cdot)$ be any generalized solution generated by

* Note, however, that they do not deal with subgame perfectness.

$\phi_i \uparrow \phi^{\text{tr}}_{-i}$, and suppose that $x^*(T) \neq \tilde{x}(T)$. By the subgame perfectness of $\hat{\phi}$ we have

$$S_i(T, x^{*1}(T)) + x_i^{*2}(T) \leqslant S_i(T, \hat{x}^1[T; \tau, x^{*1}(\tau)]) + \hat{x}_i^2[T; \tau, x^{*1}(\tau)] \tag{2.58}$$

where

$$\tau := \inf\{\tau \mid \|x^*(t) - \tilde{x}(t)\| \neq 0\} \tag{2.59}$$

Since $\hat{x}[T; \tau, \xi]$ is a continuous function of ξ, we have

$$\hat{x}[T; \tau, x^{*1}(\tau)] = \hat{x}[T; \tau, \tilde{x}^1(\tau)] \tag{2.60}$$

From relations (2.57), (2.58), and (2.60) it follows that ϕ^{tr} is an equilibrium. But this equilibrium is certainly subgame perfect. (Why?) ∎

Some subtleties are involved when $\hat{\phi}$ is discontinuous. The conclusion of Theorem 2.5 remains, however, valid.

The salient feature of the subgame perfect, feedback equilibrium, $\hat{\phi}$, is that it defines [by the inequality (2.57)] a set of *enforceable* outcomes. Under these circumstances (enforceable) cooperative (i.e., Pareto-efficient) outcomes can be achieved by a noncooperative equilibrium of strategies. This approach offers a credible alternative to the direct extensions[40,41,15] of bargaining schemes to N-person differential games. Due to their normal form presentation, solutions derived from bargaining schemes do not necessarily satisfy strategic features of extensive play. We refer the reader to Haurie[42] for an illustration of this serious weakness.

Exercises

2.1. Design a generalization of Friedman's approximation procedure in Section 2.1.3 to the case of discontinuous induced l.d.r. adapted to the following extensive situations of hierarchical play:

(a) $N=3$; $\mathscr{I}_1(t)=\{x(t)\}$; $\mathscr{I}_2(t)=\{x(t), u_1(t)\}$; $\mathscr{I}_3(t)=\{x(t), u_1(t)\}$.

(b) $N=3$; $\mathscr{I}_1(t)=\{x(t)\}$; $\mathscr{I}_2(t)=\{x(t)\}$; $\mathscr{I}_3(t)=\{x(t), u_1(t), u_2(t)\}$.

(c) $N=3$; $\mathscr{I}_1(t)=\{x(t)\}$; $\mathscr{I}_2(t)=\{x(t), u_1(t)\}$; $\mathscr{I}_3(t)=\{x(t), u_1(t), u_2(t)\}$.

2.2. Prove the second claim in Lemma 2.1.

2.3. Utilize Remark 2.4 to find Pareto-efficient outcomes for Lancaster's game of capitalism.

2.4. Using Theorems 2.2 and 2.3 find open-loop equilibria for Lancaster's game of capitalism with

(a) $l=0$; $b<1/2$,

(b) $l>1$; $b\geqslant 1/2$,

(c) $l>1$; $b<1/2$.

2.5. Prove in the general situation of Theorem 2.3 that different C^2-diffeomorphisms give birth to equilibrium candidates with different outcome and state values. Are there any exceptions to this rule?

2.6. Use Theorem 2.4 to derive the subgame perfect equilibrium (2.39a,b).

2.7. Prove (the missing step in the proof of Theorem 2.5) that ϕ^{tr} is subgame perfect.

(*Hint:* Choose $t<T$ and note that each outcome history over $[t_0, t)$ gives birth to a new initial state $y(t)$ of the remaining subgame. Analyze the two possible situations $y(t)=0$ and $y(t)\neq 0$.)

3
Methods of Solution

("That's exactly the method" the Bellman bold
In a hasty parenthesis cried,
"That's exactly the way I have always been
told
That the capture of Snarks should be tried!")

Lewis Caroll

Further conditions have to be added to those of Theorems 2.2, 2.3, and 2.4 if more is assumed about the structure of the differential game or its extensive situation.

This chapter is devoted to a presentation of necessary and sufficient conditions for equilibria in generalized differential games under simultaneous and hierarchical play. We shall furthermore illustrate how these techniques of analysis could be used to deduce solutions to dynamic situations of conflict.

3.1. Simultaneous Play

Example 3.1 (Continuation of Example 2.3.). In Chapter 2 we derived an open-loop, subgame-perfect equilibrium for Lancaster's game of capitalism. There are, however, other equilibria satisfying equations (2.36a, b). Let $\bar{t} > 0, b > 1/2$, and consider the pair of strategies* (2.39a) and

$$\tilde{\phi}_2^*(t, x) = \begin{cases} 0 & \text{if } \tilde{\eta}_2(t)\, x/x_0 - 1 \leqslant 0 \\ 1 & \text{otherwise} \end{cases} \tag{3.1a}$$

* The term decision rules would be more adequate. In accordance with the literature on differential games, we allow this sloppy formulation.

with $\tilde{\eta}_2(\cdot)$ given by

$$\tilde{\eta}_2(t) = \begin{cases} \exp[-a(1-c)(2t-\bar{t})] & \text{if } t \leqslant \bar{t} \\ a(1-b)\exp[-a(1-c)\,\bar{t}](T-t) & \text{otherwise} \end{cases} \tag{3.1b}$$

Define by

$$y_1 = x; \qquad y_2 = x^2 \tag{3.2}$$

diffeomorphisms on $X = (0, \infty)$. Starting from the pair of control values

$$\hat{u}_1^*(v_1, 2v_2x); \qquad \hat{u}_2^*(2v_2x) \tag{3.3}$$

described in equations (2.34a,b), we could show that the strategies (2.39a) and (3.1a) satisfy the maximum principle equations with costate functions $\lambda_i(\cdot)$ given by

$$\dot{\lambda}_1(t) = \begin{cases} -ab & \text{if } t > \bar{t} \\ -ac - \lambda_1(t)\,a(1-c) & \text{otherwise} \end{cases} \qquad \lambda_1(T) = 0 \tag{3.4a}$$

$$\lambda_2(t) = \begin{cases} a(1-b)(T-\bar{t})\exp[a(1-c)(\bar{t}-t)] & \text{if } t \leqslant \bar{t} \\ a(1-b)(T-t) & \text{otherwise} \end{cases} \tag{3.4b}$$

only if

$$\lambda_1(\bar{t}+0) > \lambda_1(\bar{t}-0) > 1 \tag{3.4c}$$

A precise jump condition for $\lambda_1(\cdot)$ at $t = \bar{t}$ can be obtained from the differential equation (2.35a) by invoking the calculus of generalized functions. We shall however avoid this rather formidable task. In order to verify that relations (2.39) and (3.1a) indeed comprise an equilibrium [and that inequality (3.4c) is not just a lucky guess], we shall use

$$\lambda_1(\bar{t}-0) = \lambda_1(\bar{t}+0)\{1 - a(1-b)\,\varepsilon \exp[a(1-c)\,\bar{t}]\} \quad (3.4d)$$

with

$$0 < \varepsilon < \frac{2b-1}{ab(1-b)} \exp[-a(1-c)\,\bar{t}] \quad (3.5)$$

as a (possibly inaccurate) jump condition. [Any jump condition satisfying relation (3.4c) will do the job.] Under these circumstances $\lambda_1(\cdot)$ is not necessarily the first player's costate function. ∎

3.1.1. Sufficiency under Generalized Constraints

Let ϕ denote a playable N-tuple of feedback strategies. The set of all state values $x(t)$, where $x(\cdot)$ is a state trajectory corresponding uniquely to the outcome

$$u_i(t) \uparrow \phi_{-i}(t, x(t))$$

will be called *attainable* by the ith player at time t (under the assumption that the other players stick to their feedback strategies ϕ_j, $j \neq i$), and will be denoted by $\mathscr{A}_t(\phi_{-i})$. Note that we do not exclude the case of state trajectories subjected to some constraints depending on the state value itself, say,

$$x(t) \in X(t) := \{x \in R^n \mid \bar{g}(t, x) \geqslant 0\} \quad (3.6)$$

where the function $\bar{g}: R \times R^n \to R^s$ is twice continuously differentiable with respect to all its arguments. Moreover, we shall admit control constraints of the type

$$u_i(t) \in U_i(t, x) := \{u_i \in R^{m_i} \mid g^i(t, u_i, x) \geqslant 0\} \quad (3.7)$$

where the functions $g^i: R \times R^{m_i} \times R^n \to R^{q_i}$ are continuously differentiable with respect to their arguments. Note that simultaneous play does not allow one player's move to depend upon the moves of all the others.

These relations make a redefinition of terms (such as *control path*, *outcome*, *state trajectory*, *playable* selection of decision rules, and *attainable* set of state values) necessary. This may be done by simply replacing the inclusions (2.6), (2.9) by their counterparts (3.7), (3.6). For differential games which terminate under special conditions, say,

$$\omega(T, x(T)) \geqslant 0; \qquad \bar{\omega}(T, x(T)) = 0 \quad (3.8)$$

where the functions $\omega: R \times R^n \to R^o$ and $\bar{\omega}: R \times R^n \to R^{\bar{o}}$ are continuously differentiable with respect to their arguments, the redefinition of terms must take the condition (3.8) into account.

Define for each $t \in [t_0, T]$ a selection of C^2-diffeomorphisms on $X^0(t)$ [an open set containing $X(t)$] by

$$y_i = F_i(t)\, G_i(x), \qquad i = 1,\dots, N \quad (3.9)$$

with $F_i(\cdot)$ denoting continuously differentiable $n \times n$ matrix-valued functions. Thus, each $F_i(t)$, $t \in [t_0, T]$ is invertible, i.e., there exists a continuously differentiable $n \times n$ matrix $F_i^{-1}(\cdot)$ on $[t_0, T]$ such that

$$F_i^{-1}(t)\, F_i(t) = I_{n \times n} \qquad \text{for all } t \in [t_0, T]$$

where

$$I_{n \times n} = \begin{pmatrix} 1 & 0 & \cdots & 0 \\ 0 & 1 & \cdots & 0 \\ \vdots & \vdots & \ddots & \vdots \\ 0 & 0 & \cdots & 1 \end{pmatrix}$$

The transformed Hamiltonians $H_i^{\mathscr{G}}$, $i = 1, \ldots, N$, are now given by

$$\begin{aligned} H_i^{\mathscr{G}}(t, y_i, u, v_i, v_{i0}) := {} & v_{i0} L_i[t, G_i^{-1}(F_i^{-1}(t)\, y_i), u] \\ & + v_i\{\dot{F}_i(t)\, G_i(F_i^{-1}(t)\, y_i) \\ & + F_i(t)\, \gamma_i[G_i^{-1}(F_i^{-1}(t)\, y_i)] \\ & \times f[t, G_i^{-1}(F_i^{-1}(t)\, y_i), u]\} \end{aligned} \qquad (3.10)$$

The scalar multipliers v_{i0} are needed for the formulation of necessary conditions in generalized differential games.

The following theorem is based on Stalford and Leitmann's[43] results on sufficient conditions.

Theorem 3.1. Let ϕ^* be a playable N-tuple of feedback strategies with unique state trajectory $x^*(\cdot)$, and suppose that there exist piecewise continuous and continuously differentiable functions $\eta_i(\cdot)$, $i = 1, \ldots, N$, on $[t_0, T]$ such that for all $i = 1, \ldots, N$, and all y_i satisfying the inclusion $G_i^{-1}(F_i^{-1}(t)\, y_i) \in \mathscr{A}_t(\phi^*_{-i})$ the following hold:

(a) For all $t \in [t_0, T]$ at which $\eta_i(\cdot)$ is continuous, and all $u_i \in U_i[t, G_i^{-1}(F_i^{-1}(t)\, y_i)]$ one has

$$H_i^{\mathscr{G}}[t, y_i^*(t), \phi^*[t, G_i^{-1}(F_i^{-1}(t)\, y_i^*(t))], \eta_i(t), 1]$$
$$- H_i^{\mathscr{G}}[t, y_i, u_i \uparrow \phi_{-i}^*[t, G_i^{-1}(F_i^{-1}(t)\, y_i)], \eta_i(t), 1]$$
$$\geqslant -\dot{\eta}_i(t)[y_i^*(t) - y_i] \tag{3.11}$$

where $y_i^*(\cdot) := F_i(\cdot)\, G_i[x^*(\cdot)]$.

(b)

$$\sum_{\tau \in \Delta_i^*} [\eta_i(\tau - 0) - \eta_i(\tau + 0)][y_i - y_i^*(\tau)] \geqslant 0 \tag{3.12}$$

where Δ_i^* denotes the finite set of time points at which the function $\eta_i(\cdot)$ is discontinuous.

(c) At terminal time one has

$$\eta_i(T)[y_i - y_i^*(T)] - S_i(T, y_i) + S_i(T, y_i^*(T)) \geqslant 0 \tag{3.13}$$

Then ϕ^* is an equilibrium.

Proof. Let $\tilde{x}(\cdot)$ denote the unique state trajectory corresponding to the playable N-tuple of feedback strategies $\phi_i \uparrow \phi_{-i}^*$. Then it follows that $\tilde{x}(t) \in \mathscr{A}_t(\phi_{-i}^*)$, and $\phi_i(t, \tilde{x}(t)) \in U_i(t, \tilde{x}(t))$ for all $t \in [t_0, T]$.

Define $\tilde{y}_i(\cdot) := F_i(\cdot)\, G_i[\tilde{x}(\cdot)]$. From (a), (b), (c), and the initial state condition there follows

$$\begin{aligned}
&\mathscr{J}_i(\phi^*) - \mathscr{J}_i(\phi_i \uparrow \phi^*_{-i}) \\
&\quad \geqslant \int_{t_0}^{T} [-\dot{\eta}_i(t)(y_i^* - \tilde{y}_i(t)) - \eta_i(t)(\dot{y}_i^*(t) - \dot{\tilde{y}}_i(t))]\, dt \\
&\qquad + \eta_i(T)(y_i^*(T) - \tilde{y}_i(T)) \\
&\quad = \eta_i(t_0)(y_i^*(t_0) - \tilde{y}_i(t_0)) \\
&\qquad + \sum_{\tau \in \Delta_i^*} [\eta_i(\tau + 0) - \eta_i(\tau - 0)] \\
&\qquad \times [y_i^*(\tau) - \tilde{y}_i(\tau)] \geqslant 0 \qquad (3.14)
\end{aligned}$$

This completes the proof. ∎

The conditions of Theorem 2.3 have now been sufficiently extended to apply to Example 3.1.

Example 3.2 (Continuation of Example 3.1.). From

$$x^*(t) = \begin{cases} x_o \exp[a(1-c)\, t] & \text{if } t \leqslant \bar{t} \\ x_0 \exp[a(1-c)\, \bar{t}] & \text{otherwise} \end{cases} \qquad (3.15)$$

we obviously have $\mathscr{J}_2(\phi_1^*, \tilde{\phi}_2^*) = \mathscr{J}_2(\phi_1^*, \phi_2^*)$, with ϕ_1^*, ϕ_2^*, and $\tilde{\phi}_2^*$ given by expressions (2.39a), (2.39b), and (3.1a), respectively. Therefore, it suffices to prove the validity of conditions presented in Theorem 3.1 for the case $i = 1$ only.

From equations (3.1a,b) and (3.15) we may show that for all $t \in [0, \bar{t}) \cup (\bar{t}, T]$, and all $x \in \mathscr{A}_t(\tilde{\phi}_2^*)$ one has

$$x \leqslant x^*(t); \qquad \tilde{\phi}_2^*(t, x) = \begin{cases} 0 & \text{if } t > \tilde{t}(x) \\ 1 & \text{otherwise} \end{cases} \qquad \tilde{t}(x) \leqslant \bar{t} \qquad (3.16)$$

The relations (3.16) imply that (a), (b), and (c) of Theorem 3.1 hold with $\eta_1(\cdot)$ given by (3.4a,d).

Note that the two equilibria (2.39a), (2.39b) and (2.39a), (3.1a) are equivalent. This exceptional case is solely due to the game's linearity with respect to control and state variables. ∎

If the solutions of the costate equations (2.31a, b) are used in place of the $\eta_i(\cdot)$, and if we admit candidates ϕ^* which are discontinuous with respect to the state variables, it will be necessary to consider a generalized version of Theorem 2.2.

3.1.2. Necessary Conditions under Generalized Constraints

Let ϕ^* denote an equilibrium of feedback strategies which is playable under the constraints (3.6)–(3.8), where we additionally assume that the state constraint (3.6) is of first order, i.e., the total derivative of $\bar{g}(t, x)$ with respect to time depends explicitly on the control variables. Suppose that:

1. There exists a finite, exhaustive decomposition of the domain $\mathscr{D}$ containing the playing space

$$\{(t, x) \mid t \in [t_0, T], x \in X(t)\}$$

   into nonintersecting subdomains $\mathscr{D}_k$, $k = 1, \ldots, K$, separated by, say, piecewise smooth *discontinuity manifolds* $\mathscr{M}_{kl} = \text{cl}\, \mathscr{D}_k \cap \text{cl}\, \mathscr{D}_l$, where $\text{cl}\, \mathscr{D}_k$ denotes the closure of $\mathscr{D}_k$.

2. On each subdomain $\mathscr{D}_k$ the functions $\phi_i^*(t, x)$, $i = 1,..., N$ are piecewise continuously differentiable with respect to time, and continuously differentiable with respect to the state variable(s).
3. On discontinuity manifolds the functions considered in (2) and their derivatives have finite left-hand and right-hand limits.

Define the players' Hamiltonian and Lagrangean functions by

$$H_i = \mu_{i0} L_i + \mu_i f, \qquad i = 1,..., N \tag{3.17a}$$

$$\Lambda_i = H_i + \bar{v}_i \bar{g} + v^i g^i, \qquad i = 1,..., N \tag{3.17b}$$

Theorem 3.2. Assume (in addition to the hypotheses stated above) that the matrices

$$\begin{pmatrix} \partial g_1^i/\partial u_i & g_1^i & \cdots & 0 \\ \vdots & \vdots & \ddots & \vdots \\ \partial g_{q_i}^i/\partial u_i & 0 & \cdots & g_{q_i}^i \end{pmatrix}, \qquad i = 1,..., N \tag{3.18}$$

have maximum rank, q_i, at $t \in [t_0, T]$, $x = x^*(t)$, and all $u_i \in U_i(t, x^*(t))$. Then there exist for each $i = 1,..., N$ constant multipliers

$$\alpha_i \in R^o, \qquad \bar{\alpha}_i \in R^{\bar{o}}, \qquad \xi_i \in R^s$$

and on every interval $(t_{l1}, t_{l2}) \subseteq [t_0, T]$, with

$$x^*(t) \in \mathscr{D}_l, \qquad l \in \{1,..., K\}, \qquad \text{for } t \in (t_{l1}, t_{l2})$$

a scalar λ_{i0}, equal to 0 or 1, a piecewise continuously differentiable costate function $\lambda_i: (t_{l1}, t_{l2}) \to R^n$, and piecewise continuous multiplier functions

$$\bar{\zeta}_i: (t_{l1}, t_{l2}) \to R^s, \qquad \zeta^i: (t_{l1}, t_{l2}) \to R^{q_i}$$

such that:

(a) The outcome value $\phi^*(t, x^*(t))$ is at each $t \in (t_{l1}, t_{l2})$, with the possible exception of the outcome's discontinuity points and of (say, finitely many) *junction* points [at which the state trajectory $x^*(\cdot)$ enters, leaves, or comes into contact with the surface $\bar{g}(t, x) = 0$], an equilibrium of

$$\langle H_1, ..., H_N; U_1(t, x), ..., U_N(t, x) \rangle$$

for $x = x^*(t)$, $\mu_{i0} = \lambda_{i0}$ and $\mu_i = \lambda_i(t)$, $i = 1, ..., N$.

(b) At the time points considered in (a) the following hold:

$$\frac{\partial \Lambda_i^*}{\partial u_i} = 0 \tag{3.19a}$$

$$\dot{\lambda}_i(t) = -\frac{\partial \Lambda_i^*}{\partial x} - \sum_{j \neq i} \frac{\partial \Lambda_i^*}{\partial u_j} \frac{\partial \phi_j^*(t, x^*(t))}{\partial x} \tag{3.19b}$$

$$\zeta^i(t) \geqslant 0, \qquad \zeta^i(t)\, g^i(t, x^*(t)) = 0 \tag{3.19c}$$

$$\bar{\zeta}_i(t) \geqslant 0, \qquad \bar{\zeta}_i(t)\, \bar{g}(t, x^*(t)) = 0 \tag{3.19d}$$

where $\partial \Lambda_i^* / \partial \cdot$ denotes the term $\partial \Lambda_i / \partial \cdot$ evaluated at t, $x = x^*(t)$, $u = \phi^*(t, x^*(t))$, $\mu_{i0} = \lambda_{i0}$, $\mu_i = \lambda_i(t)$, $\bar{v}_i = \bar{\zeta}_i(t)$, and $v^i = \zeta^i(t)$.

(c) At junction points $\tau^l \in (t_{l1}, t_{l2})$ there may occur discontinuities of the following kind:

$$\lambda_i(\tau^l - 0) = \lambda_i(\tau^l + 0) + \theta_i(\tau^l)\,\frac{\partial \bar{g}(\tau^l, x^*(\tau^l))}{\partial x} \tag{3.19e}$$

$$H_i^*[\tau^l - 0] = H_i^*[\tau^l + 0] - \theta_i(\tau^l)\,\frac{\partial \bar{g}(\tau^l, x^*(\tau^l))}{\partial t} \tag{3.19f}$$

$$\theta_i(\tau^l) \geqslant 0, \qquad \theta_i(\tau^l)\,\bar{g}(\tau^l, x^*(\tau^l)) = 0 \tag{3.19g}$$

where $H_i^*[t]$ denotes the evaluation of H_i at t, $x^*(t)$, $\phi^*(t, x^*(t))$, λ_{i0}, and $\lambda_i(t)$.

(d) If there exists an $\bar{\varepsilon} > 0$ such that $x^*(t) \in \mathscr{D}_j$, $j \in \{1, \ldots, K\}$, for $t \in [T - \bar{\varepsilon}, T]$, then:

$$\lambda_i(T) = \lambda_{i0}\,\frac{\partial S_i(T, x^*(T))}{\partial x} + \xi_i\,\frac{\partial \bar{g}(T, x^*(T))}{\partial x} + \alpha_i\,\frac{\partial \omega(T, x^*(T))}{\partial x} + \bar{\alpha}_i\,\frac{\partial \bar{\omega}(T, x^*(T))}{\partial x} \tag{3.19h}$$

$$\xi_i \geqslant 0, \qquad \xi_i\,\bar{g}(T, x^*(T)) = 0 \tag{3.19i}$$

$$\alpha_i \geqslant 0, \qquad \alpha_i \omega_i(T, x^*(T)) = 0 \tag{3.19j}$$

(e) At all $t \in (t_{l1}, t_{l2})$ the following nontriviality conditions hold:

$$(\lambda_{i0}, \lambda_i(t_{l2} - 0), \zeta_i(t), \theta_i(\tau_1^l), \theta_i(\tau_2^l), \ldots) \neq 0 \tag{3.19k}$$

On (t_{j1}, T) the term $\lambda_i(T-0)$ may be replaced by the row vectors ξ_i, α_i, and $\bar{\alpha}_i$.

Remark 3.1. We omit the proof which is beyond the scope of our work. We refer to Berkovitz,[44] Blaquière *et al.*,[45] Leitmann,[46] and Sarma *et al.*[47] for a rigorous derivation of necessary conditions. Highly readable presentations of necessary conditions in the realm of optimal control theory are given in Feichtinger and Hartl[32] and Seierstad and Sydsæter.[33]

Note that the conditions presented above are only almost necessary, i.e., we exclude rare cases where the occurrence of discontinuities of type (3.19e) is possible not only at junction points, but also at finitely (or even countably) many time points $t \in (t_{l1}, t_{l2})$ at which the state constraint is active.

A method of solution based on Theorem 3.2 will be practicable only if (a)–(e) may be assembled into a full picture of necessary conditions over (t_0, T) (with unique terms $\lambda_{i0}, \lambda_i(\cdot)$, etc.), where the nontriviality conditions are strengthened to $(\lambda_{i0}, \lambda_i(t)) \neq 0$. The latter assumption holds, e.g., if the functions $\bar{g}(T, \cdot)$, $\omega(T, \cdot)$, and $\bar{\omega}(T, \cdot)$ satisfy a *constraint qualification** with respect to x.

In Example 3.1, the state trajectory $x^*(\cdot)$ crosses the discontinuity manifold

$$\tilde{\eta}_2(t)\, x/x_0 = 1 \tag{3.20}$$

* This term has been defined in Section 1.3.2. See Seierstad and Sydsæter,[33] Chapter 5, for a rigorous treatment of nontriviality conditions and constraint qualifications in the framework of optimal control theory.

at $t = \bar{t}$. According to Isaacs's[(2)] nomenclature, relation (3.20) is a *transition line*. The applicability of Theorem 3.2 is, however, not restricted to such simple constellations.

Example 3.3. Consider the model of strike negotiation as posed in Section 1.2.3. For convenience we define a new state variable $x := x_2 - x_1$. The game (1.10)–(1.13) now becomes

$$\max_{u_i} \int_{t_0}^{t_f} (-a_i - u_i x)\, dt; \qquad i = 1, 2 \tag{3.21a}$$

subject to the state equation

$$\dot{x} = -(u_1 + u_2)\, x; \qquad x(t_0) = x_0 = x_{02} - x_{01} \tag{3.21b}$$

the control constraints

$$0 < b_i \leqslant u_i \leqslant 1 \tag{3.21c}$$

the state constraints

$$0 \leqslant x \leqslant x_0 \tag{3.21d}$$

and, finally,

$$t_f := \min\{t \geqslant t_0 \mid m - x(t) = 0\} \tag{3.21e}$$

The case of a terminal condition of type (3.21e) has not been dealt with in Theorem 3.2. Replace functional (3.21a) by

$$\max_{u_i, T_i} \int_{t_0}^{T_i} (-a_i - u_i x)\, dt, \qquad i = 1, 2 \tag{3.21f}$$

and condition (3.21e) by

$$\bar{\omega}(T_i, x(T_i)) = m - x(T_i) = 0, \qquad i = 1, 2; \qquad T_1 = T_2 \tag{3.21g}$$

The players' terminal time points, T_i, $i = 1, 2$, are additional control variables for this new game (which is, of course, equivalent to the original one). Suppose that an optimal terminal point $T_i = T^*$ for $i = 1, 2$ exists. Then the following condition holds (in terms of a generalized differential game satisfying the assumptions of Theorem 3.2):

$$H_i^*[T^*] - \lambda_{i0} \frac{\partial S_i(T^*, x^*(T^*))}{\partial T} - \bar{\xi}_i \frac{\partial \bar{g}(T^*, x^*(T^*))}{\partial T} - \alpha_i \frac{\partial \omega(T^*, x^*(T^*))}{\partial T} - \bar{\alpha}_i \frac{\partial \bar{\omega}(T^*, x^*(T^*))}{\partial T} = 0 \tag{3.22}$$

Define by $y = -\ln x$ a diffeomorphism on $(0, \infty)$. The condition (3.21e) [and, equivalently, (3.21f, g)] implies that $x \geqslant 0$ is not binding over $[t_0, T^*]$. We may, therefore, replace (3.21d) by

$$\exp(-y) \leqslant x_0 \tag{3.21h}$$

The players' (transformed) Hamiltonians and Lagrangeans are given by

$$H_i^{\mathscr{G}} = -\mu_{i0}(a_i + u_i \exp(-y)) + \mu_i(u_1 + u_2); \qquad i = 1, 2 \tag{3.23a}$$

$$\Lambda_i^{\mathscr{G}} = H_i^{\mathscr{G}} + \bar{v}_i(x_0 - \exp(-y)); \qquad i = 1, 2 \tag{3.23b}$$

Since the control constraints (3.21c) do not depend on the state variable, there is no need to adjoin corresponding terms to the Lagrangean functions. However, the condition (3.19a) is not valid under these circumstances.

The pair of control values

$$\hat{u}_i(\mu_{i0}, \mu_i, y) = \begin{cases} 1 & \text{if } -\mu_{i0}\exp(-y) + \mu_i > 0 \\ d_i & \text{if } -\mu_{i0}\exp(-y) + \mu_i = 0; \quad i = 1, 2 \\ b_i & \text{otherwise} \end{cases} \tag{3.24}$$

is at each t [and for arbitrary $(d_1, d_2) \in [b_1, 1] \times [b_2, 1]$] an equilibrium of the (transformed) Hamiltonian game.

At T^* the state constraint (3.21h) is not binding. In view of relation (3.21e) we obtain from equation (3.19h)

$$\lambda_i(T^*) = \bar{\alpha}_i \frac{\partial}{\partial y}[m - \exp(-y^*(T^*))] = \bar{\alpha}_i m; \ \bar{\alpha}_i \in R, \ i = 1, 2 \tag{3.25}$$

The scalar multipliers $\bar{\alpha}_i$ may be further constrained by using relation (3.22), i.e.,

$$-\lambda_{i0}(\alpha_i + \hat{u}_i[T^*]\, m) + \lambda_i(T^*)(\hat{u}_1[T^*] + \hat{u}_2[T^*]) = 0 \tag{3.26}$$

where $\hat{u}_k[T^*]$, $k = 1, 2$, denotes the control value $\hat{u}_k(\lambda_{i0}, \lambda_i(T^*), y^*(T^*))$.

In order to facilitate present exposition, we shall concentrate on the following special, symmetric case:

$$\lambda_{i0} = \lambda_0, \quad b_i = b, \quad m < a_i = a < x_0, \quad \bar{\alpha}_i = \bar{\alpha} > \lambda_0; \quad i = 1, 2 \tag{3.27}$$

From equations (3.24)–(3.26) and the nontriviality condition (3.19k) we obtain the unique value

$$\bar{\alpha} = (a + m)/(2m) \tag{3.28}$$

It may be shown that there exist state, control, and multiplier values [which do not necessarily satisfy the constraints (3.21c, d)] such that the relations

$$-\mu_{i0} \exp(-y) + \mu_i = 0; \qquad i = 1, 2 \tag{3.29}$$

hold over $[t_0, T^*]$. Let $\mu_{i0} = 1$, $u_i = \tilde{\phi}(t, y)$, $\mu_i(T^*) = \bar{\alpha} m = (a + m)/2$, and consider the differential equations

$$\dot{\mu}_i = -\frac{\partial \tilde{\Lambda}_i^{\mathscr{G}}}{\partial y} - \frac{\partial \tilde{\Lambda}_i^{\mathscr{G}}}{\partial u_j} \frac{\partial \tilde{\phi}_j(t, y)}{\partial y}; \quad j \neq i; \quad i, j = 1, 2 \tag{3.30}$$

where $\partial \tilde{\Lambda}_i^{\mathscr{G}}/\partial \cdot$ denotes the term $\partial \Lambda_i^{\mathscr{G}}/\partial \cdot$ evaluated at t, y, $u_k = \tilde{\phi}_k(t, y)$; $k = 1, 2$, $\mu_{i0} = 1$, and $\bar{v}_i = 0$. From equations (3.29) and (3.30) we get

$$\dot{\mu}_i = -\exp(-y)\, \dot{y} = -\tilde{\phi}_i(t, y) \exp(-y) - \mu_i \frac{\partial \tilde{\phi}_j(t, y)}{\partial y} \tag{3.31}$$

Evidently, we obtain the following partial differential equations:

$$0 = \exp(-y) \left[\tilde{\phi}_j(t, y) - \frac{\partial \tilde{\phi}_j(t, y)}{\partial y} \right]; \qquad j = 2, 1 \tag{3.32}$$

A possible, symmetric solution to equation (3.32) is

$$\tilde{\phi}_j(t, y) = c \exp(y); \qquad j = 2, 1 \tag{3.33}$$

where c denotes an arbitrary constant. The state trajectory $\tilde{y}(\cdot)$ corresponding to solution (3.33) is given by

$$\tilde{x}(t) = \exp(-\tilde{y}(t)) = 2c(T^* - t) + (a + m)/2 \tag{3.34}$$

Recall the costate equation from relation (3.19b). Since $\lambda_i(T^*) > \exp(-y^*(T^*)) = m$, we have $\lambda_{i0} = 1$, and $u_i = 1$; $i = 1, 2$, over a certain interval $(\tilde{t}, T^*]$. At each $t \in (\tilde{t}, T^*]$ we have

$$x^*(t) = \exp(-y^*(t)) = m \exp[2(T^* - t)] \tag{3.35}$$

Suppose that $x^*(t) < x_0$ for all $t \in (\tilde{t}, T^*]$. Then we have at each such t

$$\zeta_i(t) = 0; \quad \lambda_i(t) = a/2 + m \exp[2(T^* - t)]/2; \quad i = 1, 2 \tag{3.36}$$

Let $\tilde{t}$ denote the instant at which x^* equals $\lambda_i(t)$. From equations (3.35) and (3.36) we may derive

$$\tilde{t} = T^* - \ln(a/m)/2; \qquad \lambda_i(\tilde{t}) = x^*(\tilde{t}) = a < x_0 \tag{3.37}$$

From relations (3.34) and (3.37) we may determine a unique value for c given by

$$c = \frac{a - m}{2 \ln(a/m)} \tag{3.38}$$

Depending on the magnitude of b and c, we may discern different decompositions of the domain containing the playing space $[t_0, T^*] \times (0, x_0]$. We shall illustrate the following two interesting subcases.

Subcase 1. $bx_0 \leqslant c \leqslant a$.
The pair of symmetric strategies

$$\phi_i^*(t, x) = \begin{cases} 1 & \text{if } x < \eta(t) \\ c/x & \text{if } x = \eta(t); \\ b & \text{otherwise} \end{cases} \qquad i = 1, 2 \quad (3.39)$$

with

$$\eta(t) = \begin{cases} m \exp[2(T^* - t)]/2 + a/2 & \text{if } t > \tilde{t} \\ 2c(\tilde{t} - t) + a & \text{otherwise} \end{cases} \quad (3.40)$$

c given by expression (3.38), and

$$T^* = t_0 + [x_0 - (a + m)/2]/(2c) \quad (3.41)$$

satisfies the necessary conditions stated in Theorem 3.2 and relation (3.26). The corresponding state trajectory is initially situated on $x = \eta(t)$, and leaves this discontinuity manifold at $\tilde{t}$.

Subcase 2. $c \leqslant a < c/b < x_0$.

The pair of symmetric strategies (3.39), with

$$\eta(t) = \frac{m \exp[2(T^* - t)]}{2} + \frac{a}{2} \qquad \text{if } t > \tilde{t}$$

$$\eta(t) = \begin{cases} 2c(\tilde{t}-t)+a & \text{if } \tilde{t} \geqslant t \geqslant \bar{t} := \tilde{t} - 1/(2b) + \dfrac{a}{2c} \\ \dfrac{c \exp[2b(\bar{t}-t)]}{2b} + \dfrac{c}{2b} & \text{otherwise} \end{cases} \tag{3.42}$$

c given by expression (3.38), and

$$T^* = t_0 + [1 + \ln(bx_0/c)]/(2\mathrm{b}) - (a+m)/(4c) \tag{3.43}$$

satisfies the necessary conditions stated in Theorem 3.2 and relation (3.26). The corresponding state trajectory enters and leaves the discontinuity manifold $x = \eta(t)$ at $\bar{t}$ and $\tilde{t}$ respectively.

The strategy pairs described in Subcase 1 and Subcase 2 do not satisfy the sufficient conditions of Theorem 3.1. Nevertheless, the corresponding outcomes may be synthesized to the following feedback equilibria over $[t_0, T^*]$:

$${}^1\hat{\phi}_i(t, x) = \begin{cases} 1 & \text{if } t > \tilde{t}; \\ c/x & \text{otherwise} \end{cases} \qquad i = 1, 2 \tag{3.39a}$$

$${}^2\hat{\phi}_i(t, x) = \begin{cases} 1 & \text{if } t > \tilde{t} \\ c/x & \text{if } \bar{t} \leqslant t \leqslant \tilde{t} \\ b & \text{otherwise} \end{cases} \qquad i = 1, 2 \tag{3.39b}$$

There remains only one thing to prove: the optimality of the final time point T^*. ∎

Remark 3.2. A generalized version of Theorem 2.4 is given in Stalford and Leitmann[43] and Vaisbord and Zhukovsky.[15] Assume that constraint (3.6) is inactive, and suppose that for each $i=1,\ldots,N$ there exists a continuous function V_i defined on $[t_0, T]\times X$ such that the conditions (1)–(3) (formulated at the beginning of Section 3.1.2) hold with ϕ^* defined by relation (2.52). If:

1. The N-tuple of feedback strategies induced on the subgame $\Gamma_{[\tau,T]}$, $x(\tau)=\xi$, by ϕ^* is playable at each $(\tau, \xi)\in(t_0, T)\times X$.
2. The equality (2.51a) holds on each subdomain $\mathscr{D}_k$ (whereby we necessarily assume that the restriction of V_i to $\mathscr{D}_k$ is smooth).
3. The relation (2.51b) holds for all state values satisfying the terminal condition (3.8).

Then ϕ^* is a subgame perfect equilibrium.

Until now we have assumed that the game is played over a finite horizon. Consider the following (generalized) *infinite horizon* differential game:

$$\max\left\{J_i=\int_{t_0}^{\infty} L_i(t, x, u_1,\ldots, u_N)\, dt\right\},\quad i=1,\ldots, N \qquad (3.44)$$

subject to constraints (2.2), (3.6), and (3.7)

The concept of playability (as introduced in Section 2.2.1) can be easily extended to an infinite horizon setting. However, the payoffs corresponding to a playable set of (say) feedback rules do not necessarily exist [i.e., the improper integrals in game (3.44) are not necessarily convergent]. Nevertheless, we may handle even such cases.

Let $\tilde{\phi}$ be a playable set of feedback rules, and denote by $\tilde{x}(\cdot)$ the corresponding state trajectory. Define by

$$\mathscr{J}_i^T(\tilde{\phi}) := \int_{t_0}^{T} L_i[t, \tilde{x}(t), \tilde{\phi}(t, \tilde{x}(t))]\, dt \qquad (3.45)$$

finite horizon payoffs. We shall say that a playable set of feedback rules, ϕ^*, is an infinite horizon equilibrium according to:

(a) Weizsäcker's[48] *overtaking* criterion, if

$$\mathscr{J}_i^T(\phi^*) \geqslant \mathscr{J}_i^T(\tilde{\phi}) \qquad (3.46a)$$

for all $i = 1,..., N$, all playable $\tilde{\phi}$, and all T larger than a given, finite horizon τ;

(b) Gale's[49] *catching up* criterion, if

$$\liminf_{T \to \infty} \mathscr{J}_i^T(\phi^*) \geqslant \liminf_{T \to \infty} \mathscr{J}_i^T(\tilde{\phi}) \qquad (3.46b)$$

for all $i = 1,..., N$, and all playable $\tilde{\phi}$;

(c) Halkin's[50] *sporadically catching up* criterion, if

$$\limsup_{T \to \infty} \mathscr{J}_i^T(\phi^*) \geqslant \limsup_{T \to \infty} \mathscr{J}_i^T(\tilde{\phi}) \qquad (3.46c)$$

for all $i = 1,..., N$, and all playable $\tilde{\phi}$.

We may now use the (sufficient and necessary) conditions of Theorems 3.1 and 3.2 to find equilibria, when there is plenty of time to win the game. While there is no necessary transversality condition (3.19h), the sufficient, terminal time relation (3.13) has to be replaced by

$$\eta_i(T)[y_i - y_i^*(T)] \geqslant 0 \qquad \text{for all } T \geqslant \tau \tag{3.47a}$$

$$\liminf_{T\to\infty} \eta_i(T)[y_i - y_i^*(T)] \geqslant 0 \tag{3.47b}$$

$$\limsup_{T\to\infty} \eta_i(T)[y_i - y_i^*(T)] \tag{3.47c}$$

for each of the above criteria, respectively.

3.2. Hierarchical Play

3.2.1. Equilibria in Two-Person Games

In the previous sections we were concerned with the case of simultaneous play. For the present we consider (two-person game) equilibria which are adapted to the following (extensive) situation of hierarchical play:

$$\mathscr{I}_1(t) = \{x(t)\}; \qquad \mathscr{I}_2(t) = \{x(t), u_1(t)\} \tag{3.48}$$

At each instant t, the first player, the *leader*, acts before the other player, the *follower*. Both players know the current state. The follower has access to additional information—the value of the leader's choice of control.

Before stating appropriate equilibrium conditions, which may as well be extended to hold under the generalized constraints of Section 3.1.1, it is useful to define the so-called *Stackelberg solution*, an interesting solution concept for normal form games.

We prefer to focus attention upon $\Xi = \langle H_1, H_2;$

$U_1, U_2\rangle$, the two-person Hamiltonian game. It is not difficult to formulate an analogue to the following definition in the more general setting of Section 2.2.1.

Definition 3.1. Let t, x, μ_1, and μ_2 be given. A pair $\hat{u} = (\hat{u}_1, \hat{u}_2)$ of actions in Ξ is called a Stackelberg solution with player 1 as the leader if the following conditions hold:

$$\inf_{u_2 \in \Psi^2(\hat{u}_1;\cdot)} H_1(t, x, \hat{u}_1, u_2, \mu_1) \geqslant \inf_{u_2 \in \Psi^2(u_1;\cdot)} H_1(t, x, u_1, u_2, \mu_1) \quad \text{for all } u_1 \in U_1 \tag{3.49a}$$

$$\hat{u}_2 \in \Psi^2(\hat{u}_1; t, x, \mu_2) \tag{3.49b}$$

where

$$\Psi^2(u_1; t, x, \mu_2) := \{\tilde{u}_2 \in U_2 \mid H_2(t, x, u_1, \tilde{u}_2, \mu_2) \geqslant H_2(t, x, u_1, u_2, \mu_2) \text{ for all } u_2 \in U_2\} \tag{3.50}$$

denotes the follower's *best response set.*

For the sake of simplicity, we confine our analysis only to those differential games which lead to unique follower's responses at the Hamiltonian level, i.e., the set (3.50) (exists and) is a singleton for each $u_1 \in U_1$. Suppose that we are given an equilibrium of strategies, $\hat{\varphi}$, defined by

$$\hat{\varphi}(t, x, u_1) = (\hat{\varphi}_1(t, x), \hat{\varphi}_2(t, x, u_1)) \tag{3.51}$$

where $\hat{\varphi}_1$ and $\hat{\varphi}_2$ are continuously differentiable functions of x and u_1, respectively. At discontinuity points $\tau \in \Delta_{\hat{\varphi}}$ [where $\Delta_{\hat{\varphi}}$ is a finite subset of (t_0, T)] each $\hat{\varphi}_i$ is assumed to be right (or left) continuous.

Theorem 3.3. Let $\hat{x}(\cdot)$ denote the unique state trajectory corresponding to selection (3.51). Then the outcome value $\hat{\varphi}[t, \hat{x}(t), \hat{\varphi}_1(t, \hat{x}(t))]$ is at each $t \in [t_0, T] - \Delta_{\hat{\varphi}}$ a Stackelberg solution (with player 1 as the leader) of Ξ for $x = \hat{x}(t)$ and $\mu_i = \hat{\lambda}_i(t)$, $i = 1, 2$, with the continuous and piecewise continuously differentiable functions $\hat{\lambda}_i(\cdot)$ satisfying

$$\dot{\hat{\lambda}}_i(t) = -\frac{\partial [H_i]^*}{\partial x} - \frac{\partial [H_i]^*}{\partial u_j} \frac{\partial [\hat{\varphi}_j]^*}{\partial x} \quad (j \neq i;\ j = 1, 2) \tag{3.52a}$$

$$\hat{\lambda}_i(T) = \frac{\partial S_i(T, \hat{x}(T))}{\partial x} \tag{3.52b}$$

on $[t_0, T] - \Delta_{\hat{\varphi}}$. (By $\partial [H_i]^*/\partial \cdot$ and $\partial [\hat{\varphi}_i]^*/\partial \cdot$ we understand the terms $\partial H_i/\partial \cdot$ and $\partial \hat{\varphi}_i/\partial \cdot$ evaluated at t, $x = \hat{x}(t)$, $u = \hat{\varphi}[t, \hat{x}(t), \hat{\varphi}_1(t, \hat{x}(t))]$, and $\mu_i = \hat{\lambda}_i(t)$.)

Proof. If we are given an equilibrium of strategies (3.51), then, by definition (2.21), the control paths $\hat{\varphi}_1(\cdot, x(\cdot))$ and $\hat{\varphi}_2[\cdot, x(\cdot), \hat{\varphi}_1(\cdot, x(\cdot))]$ are optimal solutions to the following control problems:

$$\max_{u_1} \int_{t_0}^{T} L_1[t, x, u_1, \hat{\varphi}_2(t, x, u_1)]\, dt + S_1(T, x(T))$$

subject to

$$\dot{x} = f[t, x, u_1, \hat{\varphi}_2(t, x, u_1)]; \qquad x(t_0) = x_0$$

and

$$\max_{u_2} \int_{t_0}^{T} L_2[t, x, \hat{\varphi}_1(t, x), u_2]\, dt + S_2(T, x(T))$$

subject to

$$\dot{x} = f[t, x, \hat{\varphi}_1(t, x), u_2]; \qquad x(t_0) = x_0$$

The maximum principle completes the proof. ∎

In order to apply Theorem 3.3, denote by $\hat{\psi}_2$ the follower's best response

$$u_2 = \hat{\psi}_2(u_1; t, x, \mu_2) \Leftrightarrow u_2 \in \Psi^2(u_1; t, x, \mu_2) \quad \text{for all } u_1 \in U_1 \tag{3.53}$$

Let

$$(\hat{u}_1(t, x, \mu_1, \mu_2), \hat{\psi}_2) \tag{3.54}$$

be a (metagame) equilibrium of ${}^2\Xi = \langle {}^2H_1, {}^2H_2; U_1, U_2^{U_1} \rangle$. Then the pair of control values

$$(\hat{u}_1(t, x, \mu_1, \mu_2), \hat{\psi}_2(\hat{u}_1(t, x, \mu_1, \mu_2); t, x, \mu_2)) \tag{3.55}$$

is a Stackelberg solution of $\Xi = \langle H_1, H_2; U_1, U_2 \rangle$. By making use of function (3.54) and the notation of Theorem 2.3, one can prove the following result:

Theorem 3.4. Suppose that

$$\hat{\varphi}_1(t, x) := \hat{u}_1(t, x, \hat{\eta}_1(t)\,\gamma_1(x), \hat{\eta}_2(t)\,\gamma_2(x)) \tag{3.56a}$$

$$\hat{\varphi}_2(t, x, u_1) := \hat{\psi}_2(u_1; t, x, \hat{\eta}_2(t)\,\gamma_2(x)) \tag{3.56b}$$

define a sufficiently smooth pair of strategies, $\hat{\varphi}$, with corresponding unique state trajectory $\hat{x}(\cdot)$, and that the functions $\hat{\lambda}_i(\cdot)=\hat{\eta}_i(\cdot)\,\gamma_i(\hat{x}(\cdot))$, $i=1, 2$, satisfy equations (3.52a,b) on $[t_0, T]-\Delta_{\hat{\varphi}}$. If the functions

$$S_i[T, G_i^{-1}(y_i(T))]$$

and

$$H_i^{\mathscr{G}}[t, y_i, \hat{\varphi}[t, G_i^{-1}(y_i), \hat{\varphi}_1(t, G_i^{-1}(y_i))], \hat{\eta}_i(t)], \qquad i=1, 2$$

are concave with respect to $y_i \in Y_i$ (at each instant $t \in [t_0, T]$), then $\hat{\varphi}$ is an equilibrium.

Proof. In view of relations (3.56a, b), the pair of control values $\hat{\varphi}[t, G_i^{-1}(y_i), \hat{\varphi}_1(t, G_i^{-1}(y_i))]$ is at each $(t, y_i) \in Y_i$ a Stackelberg solution of $\mathscr{G}(\Xi)$ for $v_i=\hat{\eta}_i(t)$. Consequently we have

$$\begin{aligned} &H_1^{\mathscr{G}}[t, y_1, \hat{\varphi}[t, G_1^{-1}(y_1), \hat{\varphi}_1(t, G_1^{-1}(y_1))], \hat{\eta}_1(t)] \\ &\qquad \geqslant H_1^{\mathscr{G}}[t, y_1, u_1, \hat{\varphi}_2(t, G_1^{-1}(y_1), u_1), \hat{\eta}_1(t)] \qquad (3.57\text{a}) \end{aligned}$$

for all $u_1 \in U_1$, and

$$\begin{aligned} &H_2^{\mathscr{G}}[t, y_2, \hat{\varphi}[t, G_2^{-1}(y_2), \hat{\varphi}_1(t, G_2^{-1}(y_2))], \hat{\eta}_2(t)] \\ &\qquad \geqslant H_2^{\mathscr{G}}[t, y_2, \hat{\varphi}_1(t, G_2^{-1}(y_2)), u_2, \hat{\eta}_2(t)] \qquad (3.57\text{b}) \end{aligned}$$

for all $u_2 \in U_2$. The equilibrium property is now proved in a similar way as in the proof of Theorem 2.3. ∎

Remark 3.3. The correspondence between metagame equilibria and Stackelberg solutions is a well known fact in static game theory. See, e.g., Moulin.[51] Başar and

Haurie[52] have extended this result to the differential (and difference) game setting by relating equilibria of type (3.51) with (so-called) *stagewise* Stackelberg solutions. These feedback representations of equilibrium (3.51) have, however, nothing in common with the *global* Stackelberg solutions to be presented in the subsequent section.

An analogue of the dynamic programming approach stated in Theorem 2.4 may be formulated as follows:

Theorem 3.5. Suppose that $\hat{V}_i$, $i=1, 2$, are smooth functions defined on $[t_0, T]\times X$, and that each $\hat{V}_i$ satisfies the partial differential equation

$$-\frac{\partial}{\partial t}\hat{V}_i(t,x) = H_i\left[t, x, \tilde{\varphi}_1(t,x), \tilde{\varphi}_2(t,x,\tilde{\varphi}_1(t,x)), \frac{\partial}{\partial x}\hat{V}_i(t,x)\right] \tag{3.58a}$$

$$\hat{V}_i(T,x)=S_i(T,x) \tag{3.58b}$$

where the strategy pair $\tilde{\varphi}=(\tilde{\varphi}_1, \tilde{\varphi}_2)$ is given by

$$\tilde{\varphi}_1(t,x) := \hat{u}_1\left(t, x, \frac{\partial}{\partial x}V_1(t,x), \frac{\partial}{\partial x}V_2(t,x)\right) \tag{3.59a}$$

$$\tilde{\varphi}_2(t,x,u_1) := \hat{\psi}_2\left(u_1; t, x, \frac{\partial}{\partial x}\hat{V}_2(t,x)\right) \tag{3.59b}$$

If the pair of strategies induced on the subgame $\Gamma_{[\tau,T]}$, $x(\tau)=\xi$, by $\tilde{\varphi}$ is playable at each $(\tau,\xi)\in(t_0,T)\times X$, then $\tilde{\varphi}$ is a subgame perfect equilibrium.

Proof. With obvious modifications the proof of Theorem 2.4 applies equally well to this case. ∎

3.2.2. The Stackelberg Solution

Quite a different problem is obtained, if the follower has an *a priori* knowledge of the leader's decision rule. Under the assumption that the leader commits himself to act according to the rule, we may seek for a Stackelberg solution of $\langle \mathscr{J}_1, \mathscr{J}_2; \mathscr{L}_1, \mathscr{L}_2 \rangle$, the normal form of Γ_T. See Cruz[53] for a survey of leader–follower concepts in the differential game literature.

Consider the following sets of loop decision rules:

$$\mathscr{L}_1 = \mathscr{U}_1; \qquad \mathscr{L}_2 = \mathscr{F}_2 \tag{3.60}$$

i.e., the leader is restricted to open-loop decision rules, while the follower may use Lipschitzean feedback rules. The leader seeks to announce an optimal rule, knowing that the follower will react on each $\sigma_1 \in \mathscr{U}_1$ by correspondingly choosing a best response $\sigma_2^r \in \mathscr{F}_2$, with

$$\mathscr{J}_2(\sigma_1, \sigma_2^r) \geqslant \mathscr{J}_2(\sigma_1, \sigma_2) \qquad \text{for all } \sigma_2 \in \mathscr{F}_2 \tag{3.61}$$

Under appropriate smoothness assumptions, the inequality (3.61) implies the following (maximum principle) relation at the Hamiltonian level:

$$\sigma_2^r(t, x(t)) = \hat{\psi}_2(\sigma_1(t); t, x(t), \lambda_2(t)) \tag{3.62}$$

with $x(\cdot)$ and $\lambda_2(\cdot)$ denoting the state and costate trajectory, respectively.

Suppose that we are given a Stackelberg solution $\bar{\sigma}$ of $\langle \mathcal{J}_1, \mathcal{J}_2; \mathcal{U}_1, \mathcal{F}_2 \rangle$, defined by

$$\bar{\sigma}(t, x) = (\bar{\sigma}_1(t), \bar{\sigma}_2(t, x)) \tag{3.63}$$

where $\bar{\sigma}_2$ is continuously differentiable with respect to x. At discontinuity points $t \in \Delta_{\bar{\sigma}}$ [where $\Delta_{\bar{\sigma}}$ is a finite subset of (t_0, T)], the functions $\bar{\sigma}_i$ are assumed to be right (or left) continuous.

Theorem 3.6. Let $\bar{x}(\cdot)$ denote the unique state trajectory corresponding to solution (3.63). Then:

(a) The equation

$$\bar{\sigma}_2(t, \bar{x}(t)) = \bar{\psi}_2(\bar{\sigma}_1(t); t, \bar{x}(t), \bar{\lambda}_2(t)) \tag{3.64}$$

holds at each $t \in [t_0, T] - \Delta_{\bar{\sigma}}$, with the continuous and continuously differentiable functions $\bar{\lambda}_2(\cdot)$ satisfying

$$\dot{\bar{\lambda}}_2(t) = -\frac{\partial}{\partial x} H_2(t, \bar{x}(t), \hat{\sigma}_1(t), u_2, \bar{\lambda}_2(t))\bigg|_{u_2 = \bar{\sigma}_2(t, \bar{x}(t))} \tag{3.65a}$$

$$\bar{\lambda}_2(T) = \frac{\partial S_2(T, \bar{x}(T))}{\partial x} \tag{3.65b}$$

on $[t_0, T] - \Delta_{\bar{\sigma}}$.

(b) The control value $u_1 = \bar{\sigma}_1(t)$ maximizes (at each $t \in [t_0, T] - \Delta_{\bar{\sigma}}$) the leader's extended Hamiltonian

$$H(t, x, \mu_2, u_1, \mu_1, \pi)$$
$$:= H_1(t, x, u_1, \hat{\psi}_2(u_1; t, x, \mu_2), \mu_1)$$
$$+ \pi\left(-\frac{\partial}{\partial x} H_2(t, x, u_1, u_2, \mu_2)\right)\bigg|_{u_2 = \hat{\psi}_2(u_1; t, x, \mu_2)} \tag{3.66}$$

for $x = \bar{x}(t)$, $\mu_2 = \bar{\lambda}_2(t)$, $\mu_1 = \bar{\lambda}_1(t)$, and $\pi = \bar{\pi}(t)$, with the continuous and continuously differentiable functions $\bar{\lambda}_1(\cdot)$ and $\bar{\pi}(\cdot)$ satisfying

$$\dot{\bar{\lambda}}_1(t) = -\frac{\partial}{\partial x} H(t, \bar{x}(t), \bar{\lambda}_2(t), \bar{\sigma}_1(t), \bar{\lambda}_1(t), \bar{\pi}(t)) \tag{3.67a}$$

$$\bar{\lambda}_1(T) = \frac{\partial S_1(T, \bar{x}(T))}{\partial x} - \bar{\pi}(T)\frac{\partial^2 S_2(T, \bar{x}(T))}{\partial x^2} \tag{3.67b}$$

$$\dot{\bar{\pi}}(t) = -\frac{\partial}{\partial \lambda_2} H(t, \bar{x}(t), \bar{\lambda}_2(t), \bar{\sigma}_1(t), \bar{\lambda}_1(t), \bar{\pi}(t)) \tag{3.67c}$$

$$\bar{\pi}(t_0) = 0 \tag{3.67d}$$

on $[t_0, T] - \Delta_{\bar{\sigma}}$.

Proof. The leader's optimal control problem can be formulated as follows:

$$\max_{u_1} \int_{t_0}^{T} L_1(t, x, u_1, u_2)\, dt + S_1(T, x(T)) \tag{3.68a}$$

subject to the state equation

$$\dot{x} = f(t, x, u_1, u_2); \qquad x(t_0) = x_0 \qquad (3.68b)$$

and to the follower's Hamiltonian level reaction

$$u_2 = \hat{\psi}_2(u_1; t, x, \lambda_2) \qquad (3.68c)$$

$$\dot{\lambda}_2 = -\frac{\partial}{\partial x} H_2(t, x, u_1, u_2, \lambda_2); \qquad \lambda_2(T) = \frac{\partial S_2(T, x(T))}{\partial x} \qquad (3.68d)$$

Note that λ_2, the follower's costate variable, will serve as an additional state variable in the leader's problem. The conditions (3.68a, b, c, d) give the conclusions of the theorem. ∎

Unlike the simultaneous and hierarchical equilibria discussed in previous sections, a Stackelberg solution fails in general to provide a stable solution at the Hamiltonian level. Moreover, the restriction of the leader's open-loop Stackelberg rule to the subgame $\Gamma_{[\tau,T]}$, with the initial state taken as $\bar{x}(\tau)$ for $0 < \tau < T$, does (in general) not satisfy the necessary condition

$$\bar{\pi}(\tau) = 0 \qquad (3.69)$$

the subgame counterpart of condition (3.67d). For this reason, the strategic feature of time consistency does not hold for a Stackelberg solution.

Exceptions to this rule are solely due to certain structural properties of the differential game under consideration. Papavassilopoulos and Cruz[54] analyzed the situation where (the outcome corresponding to) a Stackelberg solution $\bar{\sigma}$ solves the following (team) optimal control problem:

$$\max_{u_1, u_2} \int_{t_0}^{T} L_1(t, x, u_1, u_2)\, dt + S_1(T, x(T)) \qquad (3.70a)$$

subject to

$$\dot{x} = f(t, x, u_1, u_2); \qquad x(t_0) = x_0 \qquad (3.70b)$$

Since, under these circumstances, the leader is not really constrained by the follower's costate equation (3.68d), the equality $\bar{\pi}(t) = 0$ holds for all $t \in [t_0, T]$.

The case where the leader's problem is actually a team optimal control problem for both the leader and the follower is, however, not the only constellation allowing for time consistency of Stackelberg solutions.

Example 3.4. Dockner *et al.*[55] consider the following "Eskimoean" fishery game—a two-person, finite horizon variant of the competitive, limited-access fishery problem presented in Section 1.2.5:

$$\max_{u_i > 0} \left\{ \int_{C}^{T} e^{-rt} [px - c_i]\, u_i\, dt + e^{-rT} S_i(x(T)) \right\} \qquad (3.71a)$$

subject to

$$\dot{x} = G(x) - u_1 x - u_2 x; \qquad x(0) = x_0 > 0 \quad (3.71b)$$

Contrary to Clark,[23] it is assumed that the market price p depends on the total biomass harvested by all producers being at the market. The inverse demand function

$$p(u_1 x + u_2 x) = \frac{1}{u_1 x + u_2 x} \tag{3.71c}$$

captures the case of an economy with fish as most important, nonsubstitutable food resource. The growth function $G(\cdot)$ is given by

$$G(x) = x(a - \rho \ln x) \tag{3.71d}$$

This form agrees with the Gompertz law of population growth. Finally, the *salvage* (or *terminal*) value is specified by

$$S_i(x(T)) = s_i \ln(x(T)) \tag{3.71e}$$

If

$$2c_1 + s_1 > c_2 + s_2 > s_1 > 0 \tag{3.72}$$

then the pair of strategies (defined by)

$$\hat{\varphi}_1(t) = \frac{(c_2 + s_2 e^{-(r+\rho)(T-t)} - s_1 e^{-(r+\rho)(T-t)})^2}{4c_1^2(c_2 + s_2 e^{-(r+\rho)(T-t)})} \tag{3.73a}$$

$$\hat{\varphi}_2(t, u_1) = \left[\frac{u_1}{c_2 + s_2 e^{-(r+\rho)(T-t)}}\right]^{1/2} - u_1 \tag{3.73b}$$

qualifies as an equilibrium of the Eskimoean game.

The outcome corresponding to strategies (3.73a, b)

is a time consistent (and subgame perfect) Stackelberg solution of the transformed game

$$\max_{u_i > 0} \left\{ \int_0^T e^{-rt} \left[\frac{1}{u_1 + u_2} - c_i \right] u_i \, dt + s_i \, y(T) \right\} \qquad (3.74a)$$

subject to

$$\dot{y} = -(r + \rho) \, y + e^{-rt}(a - u_1 - u_2); \qquad y(0) = \ln x_0 \qquad (3.74b)$$

This follows immediately from Theorem 3.6, and the functional form of the follower's costate equation

$$\dot{\lambda}_2(t) = (r + \rho) \, \lambda_2(t); \qquad \lambda_2(T) = s_2 \qquad (3.75)$$

which is independent of state and control variables. The original (Eskimoean) game, however, does not admit a time consistent Stackelberg solution. ∎

A leader's time inconsistent Stackelberg strategy is credible under precommitment only. In many applications, however, such commitments would constrain future policy makers. This "time-consistency" problem has received considerable attention in the literature on macroeconomic planning.*

Remark 3.4. The consideration of an extended leader's set of decision rules, say, $\mathscr{F}_1$ results in a nonclassical problem (see Papavassilopoulos and Cruz[54]).

* Pohjola[56] provides full coverage of this relevant topic.

This is due to the fact that the partial derivative of the leader's strategy with respect to the state appears in the follower's costate equation as an additional, singular control term.

Başar and Olsder[57] proposed an indirect approach that may lead, under rather restrictive conditions, to a (Lipschitzean) Stackelberg solution of $\langle \mathscr{I}_1, \mathscr{I}_2; \mathscr{F}_1, \mathscr{F}_2 \rangle$. Their method will be discussed in Section 4.1.2.

Exercises

3.1. Derive the results of Example 3.2 in detail.

3.2. Use Theorem 3.1 to show that the feedback strategies (3.39a, b) constitute an equilibrium of the strike negotiation game over $[t_0, T^*]$. Is this equilibrium subgame perfect?

3.3. Generalize Theorem 3.3 to the case of equilibria adapted to the following extensive situations of hierarchical play:
(a) $N=3$; $\mathscr{I}_1(t)=\{x(t)\}$; $\mathscr{I}_2(t)=\{x(t), u_1(t)\}$; $\mathscr{I}_3(t)=\{x(t), u_1(t)\}$.
(b) $N=3$; $\mathscr{I}_1(t)=\{x(t)\}$; $\mathscr{I}_2(t)=\{x(t)\}$; $\mathscr{I}_3(t)=\{x(t), u_1(t), u_2(t)\}$.
(c) $N=3$; $\mathscr{I}_1(t)=\{x(t)\}$; $\mathscr{I}_2(t)=\{x(t), u_1(t)\}$; $\mathscr{I}_3(t)=\{x(t), u_1(t), u_2(t)\}$.

3.4. Construct a Hamiltonian metagame for each of the extensive situations described in Exercise 3.3, and make use of the corresponding metagame equilibria to generalize Theorem 3.4.

3.5. Recall the Eskimoean fishery game of Example 3.4. Assume that condition (3.72) holds, and compare the (unique) open-loop equilibrium with the hierarchical equilibrium (3.73a,b). In which one (of two extensive situations) does the first (the second) player attain a better performance?

3.6. Prove that (3.73a, b) is indeed a hierarchical equilibrium of the Eskimoean game.
(*Hint*: Take $y_{(i)} = e^{-rt} \ln x, i = 1, 2$, and apply Theorem 3.4.)

3.7. Recall Lancaster's game of capitalism. Deduce the Stackelberg solution with
(a) capitalists
(b) workers
acting as the leader by utilizing Theorem 3.6. Compare these solutions with the open-loop equilibrium (2.39a,b). In which one (of three extensive situations) do the capitalists (the workers) attain a better performance?
(*Hint*: Pohjola[(58)].)

4
Typologies of Differential Games

> Ornithologists know all about the bird
> But their nomenclature is absurd.
>
> Ogden Nash

In this chapter, we shall attempt to give a (rudimentary) classification of differential games. There are different schemes that may reveal similarities among games. To begin with, the most simple typology reflects the structure of a differential game as represented by the players' payoffs and the dynamic state equation. Differential games with linear state differential equations and quadratic performance criteria will be introduced in Section 4.1.

Clemhout and Wan,[(59)] Leitmann and Schmitendorf,[(60)] and Reinganum[(61)] isolated different tractable (classes of) games, whose open-loop equilibria are subgame perfect. The typological connection between their classes of games has been investigated by Mehlmann and Willing,[(62)] but the main criterion which made it obvious is due to Fershtman.[(63)] Section 4.2 will be devoted to a presentation of these *perfect* games.

Only rarely is it possible to obtain explicit solutions to differential games. For certain classes of games, diagrammatic analysis provides a qualitative characterization of solutions which are not explicitly derivable from the maximum principle. Section 4.3 deals with such *qualitatively solvable* games.

4.1. Linear-Quadratic Games

Consider the following (two-person) differential game:

$$\max_{u_i \in R^{m_i}} \frac{1}{2} \left\{ \int_{t_0}^{T} x' Q_i(t)\, x + \sum_{j=1}^{2} u_j' S_{ij}(t)\, u_j\, dt + x'(T)\, Q_i^{(T)} x(T) \right\} \tag{4.1a}$$

subject to

$$\dot{x} = A(t)\, x + \sum_{i=1}^{2} B_i(t)\, u_i; \qquad x(t_0) = x_0 (\in R^n) \tag{4.1b}$$

The functions $A(\cdot)$, $B_i(\cdot)$, $Q_i(\cdot)$, and $S_{ij}(\cdot)$ are matrix-valued and, say, continuous with respect to time. The real matrices $Q_i(t)$, $Q_i^{(T)}$, and $S_{ij}(t)$ are symmetric for all $t \in [t_0, T]$. We shall moreover assume that the $n \times n$ matrices $S_{ii}(t)$ are negative definite [in symbolic notation $S_{ii}(t) < 0$] for $i = 1, 2$ and all $t \in [t_0, T]$.

4.1.1. *Affine Equilibria*

Define an affine pair of feedback strategies ψ^* by

$$\psi_i^*(t, x) := -S_{ii}^{-1} B_i' [(P_i + F_i)\, x - F_i x^* + v_i]; \quad i = 1, 2 \tag{4.2}$$

Let $F_i(\cdot)$, $P_i(\cdot)$ denote real $n \times n$ matrix-valued functions which are differentiable with respect to time, and assume that the $P_i(\cdot)$ satisfy the following system of coupled differential equations:

$$
\begin{aligned}
-\dot{P} &= \tilde{A}'P + P\tilde{A} + (1-\kappa)\,Q - PSP - (1-\omega)\,PJSPJ \\
&\qquad - (1-\delta)(JPSJP - JPJS_0JPJ) \\
P(T) &= (1-\kappa)\,Q^{(T)}
\end{aligned}
\tag{4.3}
$$

where κ, ω, $\delta \in [0, 1]$, and

$$
\tilde{A} = \begin{pmatrix} A & 0 \\ 0 & A \end{pmatrix}; \qquad Q^{(T)} = \begin{pmatrix} Q_1^{(T)} & 0 \\ 0 & Q_2^{(T)} \end{pmatrix};
$$

$$
Q = \begin{pmatrix} Q_1 & 0 \\ 0 & Q_2 \end{pmatrix}
$$

$$
S = \begin{pmatrix} B_1 S_{11}^{-1} B_1' & 0 \\ 0 & B_2 S_{22}^{-1} B_2' \end{pmatrix};
$$

$$
S_0 = \begin{pmatrix} B_2 S_{22}^{-1} S_{12} S_{22}^{-1} B_2' & 0 \\ 0 & B_1 S_{11} S_{21} S_{11}^{-1} B_1' \end{pmatrix}
$$

$$
P = \begin{pmatrix} P_1 & 0 \\ 0 & P_2 \end{pmatrix}; \qquad J = \begin{pmatrix} 0 & I \\ I & 0 \end{pmatrix};
$$

$$
I = \text{the } n \times n \text{ identity matrix}
$$

Let the n-dimensional vector-valued functions $v_i(\cdot)$ be given by the following differential equation:

$$
\begin{aligned}
\dot{v} &= (PS + PJS - \tilde{A}' + J(P + F')\,SJ - J(P + F')\,JS_0J)\,v \\
&\qquad + (J(\delta P + F')\,SJP - J(\delta P + F')\,JS_0JP \\
&\qquad - \kappa Q + \omega PJSPJ)\,y^* \\
v(T) &= \kappa Q^{(T)} y^*(T)
\end{aligned}
\tag{4.4}
$$

where

$$F=\begin{pmatrix} F_1 & 0 \\ 0 & F_2 \end{pmatrix}; \quad v=\begin{pmatrix} v_1 \\ v_2 \end{pmatrix}; \quad y^*=\begin{pmatrix} x^* \\ x^* \end{pmatrix}$$

and

$$\dot{y}^*=(\tilde{A}-SP-JSP)\,y^*-(S+JS)\,v; \quad y^*(t_0)=(x_0', x_0')' \tag{4.5}$$

Let $\Phi_M(s, t)$ denote the fundamental solution of the linear differential equation

$$(d/dt)\begin{pmatrix} y^* \\ v \end{pmatrix}=\begin{pmatrix} M_{11} & M_{12} \\ M_{21} & M_{22} \end{pmatrix}\begin{pmatrix} y^* \\ v \end{pmatrix} \tag{4.6}$$

where the matrices $M_{ij}(t)$ are defined by the corresponding terms in equations (4.4) and (4.5). Divide the $4n \times 4n$ matrix $\Phi_M(s, t)$ into $n \times n$ submatrices

$$\Phi_M(s, t)=(\Phi_{kl}(s, t))_{k,l=0,1,2,3}$$

If we knew, instead of the initial state value x_0, the final state value $x(T)=x_T$, then the unique state trajectory corresponding to expression (4.2) would be given by

$$x^*(t)=(\Phi_{00}(t, T)+\kappa \sum_{j=2}^{3} \Phi_{0j}(t, T)\, Q_j^{(T)})\, x_T \quad \text{for al } t \in [t_0, T] \tag{4.7}$$

Using this relation, we obtain the following result:

Theorem 4.1. Suppose that

(a) the matrix $\Phi_{00}(t_0, T) + \kappa \sum_{j=2}^{3} \Phi_{0j}(t_0, T)\, Q_j^{(T)}$ is invertible,

(b) the differential system (4.3) has a solution on $[t_0, T]$,

(c) the matrices $Q^{(T)}$ and

$$Q + J(P + F')\, JS_0 J(P + F)\, J \tag{4.8}$$

are negative semidefinite (in symbolic notation $\leqslant 0$) for all $t_0 \leqslant t \leqslant T$.

Then the feedback strategies (4.2) constitute an equilibrium of the linear-quadratic differential game under consideration.

Proof. If the first two conditions hold, we obtain, for each solution $P(\cdot)$ of system (4.3), unique continuously differentiable solutions $v(\cdot)$ of system (4.4), and $y^*(\cdot)$ of equation (4.5) over $[t_0, T]$. Therefore, the pair of feedback l.d.r. (4.2) is playable.

At each $t \in [t_0, T]$ the outcome corresponding to solution (4.2) is a Hamiltonian game equilibrium for $x = x^*(t)$ and $\mu_i = \lambda_i(t) := (P_i(t)\, x^*(t) + v_i(t))'$. It is now readily verified that solution (4.2) satisfies the necessary conditions stated in Theorem 2.2. The last part of the proof follows (by standard application of Theorem 3.1) from condition (c). ∎

Note that even if system (4.3) is uniquely solvable, different $F_i(\cdot)$ give birth to different state trajectories $x^*(\cdot)$. This illustrates Başar's[64] result on the occurrence of (uncountable many) "informationally" nonunique equilibria in differential games. There are, however, two exceptions to this rule. (For the discrete time case, see Başar and Selbuz.[65])

Theorem 4.2. Suppose that the linear-quadratic game is a team problem or a zero-sum game. Then each choice of $F_i(\cdot)$ (for $i=1, 2$) leads to the same fundamental solution $\Phi_M(s, t)$ (and *vice versa*).

Proof. Without loss of generality, the two degenerate cases of a team problem and a zero-sum game can be identified with

$$S = JS_0J; \qquad P = JPJ; \qquad Jv = v \tag{4.9}$$

or

$$S = -JS_0J; \qquad P = -JPJ; \qquad Jv = -v \tag{4.10}$$

respectively. Bearing in mind that $y^* = Jy^*$, it may be shown that equation (4.6) does not depend on the choice of $F_i(\cdot)$, $i=1, 2$, if (and only if) conditions (4.9) or (4.10) are satisfied. ∎

By setting

$$\kappa = 1; \qquad \omega = 1; \qquad \delta = 1; \qquad F = 0 \tag{4.11}$$

in relations (4.2)–(4.5), we obtain conditions for the existence of a unique open-loop equilibrium. For an alternative approach, see Eisele.[66]

Theorem 4.3. The linear-quadratic differential game (4.1a, b) with $Q^{(T)} \leqslant 0$ and $Q(t) \leqslant 0$ for all $t \in [t_0, T]$ admits (for any initial state value $x_0 \in R^n$) a unique open-loop equilibrium if (and only if) the matrix $\Phi_{00}(t_0, T) + \sum_{j=2}^{3} \Phi_{0j}(t_0, T)\, Q_j^{(T)}$ corresponding to conditions (4.11) is invertible.

Proof. Under assumption (4.11), the differential system (4.3) is a special *matrix-Riccati* differential equation which admits $P(t) = 0$ for all $t \in [t_0, T]$ as unique solution. Since the conditions (a)–(c) of Theorem 4.1 are satisfied,

$$\psi_i^*(t) = -S_{ii}^{-1} B_i' v_i; \qquad i = 1, 2 \tag{4.12}$$

is an equilibrium for any initial state value. Solution (4.12) is the only open-loop candidate satisfying the necessary conditions of Theorem 2.2, if, and only if,

$$\Phi_{00}(t_0, T) + \sum_{j=2}^{3} \Phi_{0j}(t_0, T)\, Q_j^{(T)}$$

[corresponding to conditions (4.11)] is invertible. ∎

Remark 4.1. Set

$$\kappa = 0; \qquad \omega = 1; \qquad \delta = 1; \qquad F = -P \tag{4.13}$$

The unique open-loop equilibrium (4.12) admits a representation

$$\psi_i^*(t) = -S_{ii}^{-1} B_i'(P_i x^* + v_i); \qquad i = 1, 2 \tag{4.14}$$

if the matrix $\Phi_{00}(t_0, T)$ corresponding to conditions (4.13) is invertible.

Under the additional assumption that $\Phi_{00}(t, T)$ is invertible for all $t \in [t_0, T]$, the open-loop equilibrium (4.14) may be written as

$$\psi_i^*(t) = -S_{ii}^{-1} B_i' \tilde{P}_i x^*; \qquad i = 1, 2 \tag{4.15}$$

where $\tilde{P}_i(\cdot)$ denotes the unique continuously differentiable solution of

$$\dot{\tilde{P}}_i = -Q_i - A'\tilde{P}_i - \tilde{P}_i A + \tilde{P}_i \sum_{j=1}^{2} B_j S_{jj}^{-1} B_j' \tilde{P}_j; \quad \tilde{P}_i(T) = Q_i^{(T)} \tag{4.16}$$

over $[t_0, T]$.

With

$$\kappa = 0; \qquad \omega = 0; \qquad \delta = 1; \qquad F = -P \tag{4.17}$$

we may as well derive the open-loop form (4.15), (4.16). In this case, we have $v = 0$ for all $t \in [t_0, T]$. Thus, the state trajectory $x^*(\cdot)$ may be obtained by solving a simple linear initial value problem. The unique solvability of system (4.3), however, is satisfied only if the matrix $\Phi_{00}(t, T)$ corresponding to conditions (4.13) is invertible for each $t \in [t_0, T)$ (see, e.g., Eisele[66]).

The result of Theorem 4.1 may be specialized to obtain a subgame perfect feedback equilibrium.

Theorem 4.4. Suppose that the $n \times n$ matrix-valued functions $\bar{P}_i(\cdot)$, $i = 1, 2$, constitute a solution to the differential system (4.3) with $\kappa = \omega = \delta = 0$. Then, the linear-quadratic game (4.1a,b) with $Q^{(T)} \leqslant 0$, $Q(t) \leqslant 0$, $S_{12}(t) \leqslant 0$, $S_{21}(t) \leqslant 0$ for all $t \in [t_0, T]$ admits a subgame perfect equilibrium in linear strategies, given by

$$\psi_i^*(t, x) = -S_{ii}^{-1} B_i' \bar{P}_i x; \qquad i = 1, 2 \tag{4.18}$$

Proof. Set

$$\kappa = 0; \qquad \omega = 0; \qquad \delta = 0; \qquad F = 0 \tag{4.19}$$

and apply Theorem 4.1 [without condition (a)]. Since $v = 0$ for all $t \in [t_0, T]$, the state equation can be solved directly. ∎

4.1.2. *Stackelberg Solutions*

Define a pair of open-loop decision rules $\hat{\psi}$ by

$$\hat{\psi}_i(t) = -S_{ii}^{-1} B_i' (\hat{P}_i \hat{x} + \hat{v}_i); \qquad i = 1, 2 \tag{4.20}$$

Assume that the $\hat{P}_i(\cdot)$, $i = 1, 2$, satisfy the following system of coupled (matrix Riccati) differential equations

$$\begin{aligned} -\dot{\hat{P}} &= \tilde{A}'\hat{P} + \hat{P}\tilde{A} + Q - \hat{P}S\hat{P} - (1-\gamma)(\hat{P}JS\hat{P}J + JQJ\tilde{K}) \\ \hat{P}(T) &= Q^{(T)} - (1-\gamma)\, JQ^{(T)}J\tilde{K}(T) \end{aligned} \tag{4.21}$$

where

$$\gamma \in [0, 1]; \quad \hat{P} = \begin{pmatrix} \hat{P}_1 & 0 \\ 0 & \hat{P}_2 \end{pmatrix}; \quad \tilde{K} = \begin{pmatrix} K & 0 \\ 0 & 0 \end{pmatrix}$$

and with $K(\cdot)$ satisfying

$$\dot{K} = -B_2 S_{22}^{-1} S_{12} S_{22}^{-1} B_2' \hat{P}_2 + B_2 S_{22}^{-1} B_2' \hat{P}_1 + AK - KA$$
$$+ K(B_1 S_{11}^{-1} B_1' \hat{P}_1 + B_2 S_{22}^{-1} B_2' \hat{P}_2); \qquad K(t_0) = 0 \tag{4.22}$$

Let the n-dimensional vector-valued functions $\hat{v}_i(\cdot)$ be given by the following differential equation:

$$\dot{\hat{v}} = (\hat{P}S + \hat{P}JS - \tilde{A}')\,\hat{v} + \gamma(\hat{P}JS\hat{P}J + JQJ\tilde{K})\,\hat{y} + JQJ\tilde{w}$$
$$\hat{v}(T) = -JQ^{(T)}J(\gamma\tilde{K}(T)\,\hat{y}(T) + \tilde{w}(T)) \tag{4.23}$$

where

$$\hat{v} = \begin{pmatrix} \hat{v}_1 \\ \hat{v}_2 \end{pmatrix}; \qquad \hat{y} = \begin{pmatrix} \hat{x} \\ \hat{x} \end{pmatrix}; \qquad \tilde{w} = \begin{pmatrix} w \\ 0 \end{pmatrix}$$

and with $w(\cdot)$ satisfying

$$\dot{w} = -B_2 S_{22}^{-1} S_{12} S_{22}^{-1} B_2' \hat{v}_2 + B_2 S_{22}^{-1} B_2' \hat{v}_1 + Aw$$
$$+ K(B_1 S_{11}^{-1} B_1' \hat{v}_1 + B_2 S_{22}^{-1} B_2' \hat{v}_2); \qquad w(t_0) = 0 \tag{4.24}$$

Function $\hat{x}(\cdot)$ denotes the state trajectory corresponding to rules (4.20), i.e.,

$$\dot{\hat{x}} = A\hat{x} - B_1 S_{11}^{-1} B_1'(\hat{P}_1 \hat{x} + \hat{v}_1) - B_2 S_{22}^{-1} B_2'(\hat{P}_2 \hat{x} + \hat{v}_2);$$
$$\hat{x}(t_0) = x_0 \tag{4.25}$$

Set $\gamma = 1$, and let $\Phi_G(s, t)$ denote the fundamental solution of the linear differential equation

$$(d/dt)\begin{pmatrix} \hat{x} \\ w \\ \hat{v}_1 \\ \hat{v}_2 \end{pmatrix} = \begin{pmatrix} G_{00} & \cdots & G_{03} \\ \vdots & \ddots & \vdots \\ G_{30} & \cdots & G_{33} \end{pmatrix}\begin{pmatrix} \hat{x} \\ w \\ \hat{v}_1 \\ \hat{v}_2 \end{pmatrix} \tag{4.26}$$

where the matrices $G_{ij}(t)$ are defined by the corresponding terms in relations (4.20)–(4.23). Divide the $4n \times 4n$ matrix $\Phi_G(s, t)$ into $n \times n$ submatrices

$$\Phi_G(s, t) = \Phi_{kl}(s, t)_{k,l=0,1,2,3}$$

Define matrices $\Theta_{ij}(s, T)$, $i = 0, 1, 2, 3$, $j = 0, 1$ by

$$\begin{aligned} \Theta_{i0}(s, T) &:= \Phi_{i0}(s, T) - \Phi_{i2}(s, T)\, Q_2^{(T)} K(T) \\ \Theta_{i1}(s, T) &:= \Phi_{i1}(s, T) - \Phi_{i2}(s, T)\, Q_2^{(T)} \end{aligned} \tag{4.27}$$

and denote by $\Theta_0(s, T)$ the matrix

$$\Theta_0(s, T) = \begin{pmatrix} \Theta_{00}(s, T) & \Theta_{01}(s, T) \\ \Theta_{10}(s, T) & \Theta_{11}(s, T) \end{pmatrix}$$

Theorem 4.5. Suppose that

$$Q^{(T)} \leqslant 0; \quad Q(t) \leqslant 0, \quad S_{12} < 0 \quad \text{for all } t \in [t_0, T] \tag{4.28}$$

and that the matrix $\Theta_0(t_0, T)$ is invertible. Then

$$\hat{\psi}_i(t) = -S_{ii}^{-1} B_i'(\hat{P}_i \hat{x} + \hat{v}_i); \qquad i = 1, 2 \tag{4.20}$$

is (for initial state value $x_0 \in R^n$) a unique open-loop Stackelberg solution of the linear-quadratic game under consideration.

Proof. Under the assumption (4.28), both the leader's and the follower's problem are uniquely solvable. Let $\Theta_0(t_0, T)$ be invertible, and denote by $\tilde{\Theta}_{ij}(t_0, T)$, $i, j = 0, 1$, the $n \times n$ submatrices of $[\Theta_0(t_0, T)]^{-1}$. Using the relations

$$\hat{x}_T := \hat{x}(T) = \tilde{\Theta}_{00}(t_0, T)\, x_0; \quad w_T := w(T) = \tilde{\Theta}_{10}(t_0, T)\, x_0$$

we may derive the following unique solution to the differential system (4.23)–(4.25):

$$\begin{aligned} \hat{x}(t) &= [\Theta_{00}(t, T)\, \tilde{\Theta}_{00}(t_0, T) + \Theta_{01}(t, T)\, \tilde{\Theta}_{10}(t_0, T)]\, x_0 \\ &= \hat{\Theta}_{00}(t, T)\, x_0 \end{aligned} \tag{4.29a}$$

$$\begin{aligned} w(t) &= [\Theta_{10}(t, T)\, \tilde{\Theta}_{00}(t_0, T) + \Theta_{11}(t, T)\, \tilde{\Theta}_{10}(t_0, T)]\, x_0 \\ &= \hat{\Theta}_{10}(t, T)\, x_0 \end{aligned} \tag{4.29b}$$

$$\begin{aligned} \hat{v}_1(t) &= [\Theta_{20}(t, T)\, \tilde{\Theta}_{00}(t_0, T) + \Theta_{21}(t, T)\, \tilde{\Theta}_{10}(t_0, T)]\, x_0 \\ &= \hat{\Theta}_{20}(t, T)\, x_0 \end{aligned} \tag{4.29c}$$

$$\begin{aligned} \hat{v}_2(t) &= [\Theta_{30}(t, T)\, \tilde{\Theta}_{00}(t_0, T) + \Theta_{31}(t, T)\, \tilde{\Theta}_{10}(t_0, T)]\, x_0 \\ &= \hat{\Theta}_{30}(t, T)\, x_0 \end{aligned} \tag{4.29d}$$

The differential equation (4.21) admits for $\gamma = 1$ a unique continuously differentiable solution on $[t_0, T]$. From equations (4.21)–(4.24), it readily follows that the playable open-loop pair (4.20) satisfies the necessary conditions stated in Theorem 3.6. Since both the leader's and the follower's Hamiltonian are strictly concave with respect to the state variables, the theorem's conclusion is verified. ∎

Remark 4.2. Simaan and Cruz[67] obtain the following representation of an open-loop Stackelberg solution

$$\hat{\psi}_i(t) = -S_{ii}^{-1} B_i' \Pi_i \hat{x}; \qquad i = 1, 2, \tag{4.30}$$

where $\Pi_i(\cdot)$ [and $\mathrm{K}(\cdot)$] denote the unique continuously differentiable solution to the differential system

$$\begin{aligned} \dot{\Pi} &= -\tilde{A}'\Pi - \Pi\tilde{A} - Q + \Pi S \Pi + \Pi J S \Pi J + JQJ\tilde{\mathrm{K}} \\ \Pi(T) &= Q^{(T)} - JQ^{(T)}J\tilde{\mathrm{K}}(T) \end{aligned} \tag{4.31a}$$

$$\begin{aligned} \dot{\mathrm{K}} = {} & -B_2 S_{22}^{-1} S_{12} S_{22}^{-1} B_2' \Pi_2 + B_2 S_{22}^{-1} B_2' \Pi_1 + A\mathrm{K} - \mathrm{K}A \\ & + \mathrm{K}(B_1 S_{11}^{-1} B_1' \Pi_1 + B_2 S_{22}^{-1} B_2' \Pi_2); \qquad \mathrm{K}(t_0) = 0 \end{aligned} \tag{4.31b}$$

We may derive this functional form directly from relations (4.20)–(4.25) by setting $\gamma = 0$. In this case, we have $\hat{v}(t) = 0$ and $w(t) = 0$ for all $t \in [t_0, T]$. Note that the unique solvability of system (4.31a, b) is only justified under the following additional assumption.

Theorem 4.6. The differential system (4.31a,b) admits a unique solution on $[t_0, T]$ if (and only if) the matrix $\hat{\Theta}_{00}(t, T)$ is invertible for all $t \in [t_0, T]$.

Proof. Let the assumptions of Theorem 4.5 hold,

and suppose that $\hat{\Theta}_{00}(t, T)$ is invertible for all $t \in [t_0, T]$. From relations (4.29a,b, c, d), we have

$$\begin{aligned} w(t) &= \hat{\Theta}_{10}(t, T)[\hat{\Theta}_{00}(t, T)]^{-1}\, \hat{x}(t) \\ \hat{v}_1(t) &= \hat{\Theta}_{20}(t, T)[\hat{\Theta}_{00}(t, T)]^{-1}\, \hat{x}(t) \\ \hat{v}_2(t) &= \hat{\Theta}_{30}(t, T)[\hat{\Theta}_{00}(t, T)]^{-1}\, \hat{x}(t) \end{aligned}$$

Thus, the matrix functions given by

$$\Pi_i(t) = \hat{P}_i(t) + \hat{\Theta}_{i+1,0}(t, T)[\hat{\Theta}_{00}(t, T)]^{-1}; \qquad i = 1, 2 \tag{4.32a}$$

$$\mathrm{K}(t) = \mathrm{K}(t) + \hat{\Theta}_{10}(t, T)[\hat{\Theta}_{00}(t, T)]^{-1} \tag{4.32b}$$

constitute a unique and continuously differentiable solution to the differential system (4.31a,b).

The necessity of the criterion can be deduced after some tedious manipulations. ∎

A naive approach toward the derivation of linear Stackelberg solutions leads to a unique follower's reaction

$$\hat{\psi}_2(t, x) = -S_{22}^{-1} B_2' \hat{\lambda}_2' = -S_{22}^{-1} B_2' P_2 x \tag{4.33}$$

with state and costate equations given by

$$\begin{aligned} \dot{x} &= (A - B_1 \hat{L}_1)\, x - B_2 S_{22}^{-1} B_2' \hat{\lambda}_2' \\ &= (A - B_1 \hat{L}_1 - B_2 S_{22}^{-1} B_2' P_2)\, x; \qquad x(t_0) = x_0 \end{aligned} \tag{4.34a}$$

$$\dot{\hat{\lambda}}_2' = \dot{P}_2 x + P_2 \dot{x}$$
$$= -(Q_2 + \hat{L}_1' S_{21} \hat{L}_1)\, x - (A - B_1 \hat{L}_1)' \hat{\lambda}_2'; \qquad (4.34b)$$
$$\hat{\lambda}_2'(T) = Q_2^{(T)} x(T)$$

The leader's problem, however, does not admit a linear solution.

The highest payoff the leader can expect to obtain is reached by the team* solution

$$\tilde{\psi}_i(t, x) = -S_{1i} B_i' \tilde{P}_x; \qquad i = 1, 2 \qquad (4.35)$$

to his own problem. The matrix function $\tilde{P}(\cdot)$ is defined as the unique solution of

$$\dot{\tilde{P}} = -Q_1 - A'\tilde{P} - \tilde{P}A + \tilde{P}(B_1 S_{11}^{-1} B_1' + B_2 S_{12}^{-1} B_2')\, \tilde{P}$$
$$\tilde{P}(T) = Q_1^{(T)} \qquad (4.36)$$

Following Başar and Olsder,[57] we may search for a representation of the leader's team strategy to which the best response coincides with the follower's team strategy. This necessarily implies that the state trajectory corresponding to this particular Stackelberg solution is precisely the trajectory $\tilde{x}(\cdot)$ generated by the team solution (4.35). The following result[57] may now be stated.

* Both players are maximizing the leader's payoff.

Theorem 4.7. Let the continuous matrix function $\tilde{M}(\cdot)$ be given so that the unique solution of

$$\begin{aligned}
&\dot{\Upsilon} + \Upsilon[A - (B_1 S_{11}^{-1} B_1' + B_2 S_{12}^{-1} B_2')\,\tilde{P}] \\
&\quad + [A - (B_1 S_{11}^{-1} B_1' + B_2 S_{12}^{-1} B_2')\,\tilde{P}]'\Upsilon \\
&\quad + \tilde{M} B_1' \Upsilon - \tilde{M} S_{21} S_{11}^{-1} B_1' \tilde{P} + Q_2 \\
&\quad + \tilde{P}(B_1 S_{11}^{-1} S_{21} S_{11}^{-1} B_1' + B_2 S_{12}^{-1} S_{22} S_{12}^{-1} B_2')\,\tilde{P} = 0; \\
&\Upsilon(T) = Q_2^{(T)}
\end{aligned} \tag{4.37}$$

satisfies the relation

$$S_{22}^{-1} B_2' \Upsilon = S_{12}^{-1} B_2' \tilde{P} \tag{4.38}$$

Then

$$\tilde{\psi}_1(t, x) = (\tilde{M}' - S_{11}^{-1} B_1' \tilde{P})\, x - \tilde{M}' \tilde{x} \tag{4.39a}$$

$$\tilde{\psi}_2(t, x) = -S_{12}^{-1} B_2' \tilde{P}_x \tag{4.39b}$$

constitutes a Stackelberg solution of the linear quadratic game under consideration.

Proof. Suppose that the leader announces the following decision rule:

$$\psi_1(t, x) = -S_{11}^{-1} B_1' \tilde{P} x + M'(x - \tilde{x}) \tag{4.40}$$

Then the follower's reaction (at the Hamiltonian level) is given by

$$-S_{22}^{-1} B_2' \lambda_2' \tag{4.41}$$

where the continuous differentiable costate function $\lambda_2(\cdot)$ is the unique solution of

$$\begin{aligned}\dot{\lambda}_2' = &-[Q_2 + (M' - S_{11}^{-1}B_1'\tilde{P})'\, S_{21}(M' - S_{11}^{-1}B_1'\tilde{P})]\, x \\ &+ (M' - S_{11}^{-1}B_1'\tilde{P})'S_{21}M'\tilde{x} \\ &- (A - B_1 S_{11}^{-1}B_1'\tilde{P} + B_1 M')'\lambda_2'; \qquad \lambda_2'(T) = Q_2^{(T)}x(T)\end{aligned} \tag{4.42}$$

over $[t_0, T]$. Under the theorem's assumptions, we obtain

$$S_{22}^{-1}B_2'\lambda_2' = S_{22}^{-1}B_2'\Upsilon\tilde{x} = S_{12}^{-1}B_2'\tilde{P}\tilde{x}$$

This completes the proof. ∎

4.2. Perfect Games

The basic feature that distinguishes the games analyzed in this section from the linear quadratic games is the subgame perfectness of open-loop equilibria (if they exist). Our presentation starts with the *trilinear* game introduced by Clemhout and Wan.[59]

4.2.1. Trilinear, State-Redundant, and Exponential Games

Consider the following N-person differential game

$$\max_{u_i \in U_i} \int_{t_0}^{T} \left\{ \left[\sum_{j=1}^{N} c_{ij}^0(u_j)\, d_j + e_i^0(t) \right] x + b_i^0(t) \right\} dt \tag{4.43a}$$

subject to

$$\dot{x} = \left(\sum_{j=1}^{N} [c_j(u_j) \otimes d_j] + E(t) \right) x + b(t) \qquad (4.43b)$$

and

$$\begin{pmatrix} d_1 \\ \vdots \\ d_N \end{pmatrix} x > 0 \qquad (4.43c)$$

where d_j is an n-dimensional row vector for $j = 1, \ldots, N$; $E(\cdot)$ is an $n \times n$ matrix valued function, $e_i^0(\cdot)$, $i = 1, \ldots, N$, and $b(\cdot)$ are n-vector valued functions, and $b_i^0(\cdot)$ are scalar functions on $[t_0, T]$. For $i, j = 1, \ldots, N$, denote by $c_j(\cdot)$ and $c_{ij}^0(\cdot)$ twice differentiable, n-vector valued and scalar valued functions, respectively, defined on compact and convex sets $U_i \subseteq R^{m_i}$. The term $c_j \otimes d_j$ denotes the matrix resulting from the multiplication of the column vector c_j by the row vector d_j.

The players' Hamiltonians are linear with respect to the state variables x, the multiplier μ_i, and the functions (c_{ij}^0, c_j) for $j = 1, \ldots, N$. This fact allows us to nickname the game trilinear. In light of inequality (4.43c), a Hamiltonian game equilibrium corresponding to a trilinear game does not depend on x.

Theorem 4.8. Suppose that

$$\hat{u}^*(\mu_1, \ldots, \mu_N) = (\hat{u}_1^*(\mu_1), \ldots, \hat{u}_N^*(\mu_N)) \qquad (4.44)$$

is a unique equilibrium of the Hamiltonian game, and suppose that the corresponding costate system (2.31a, b) with $\phi_i^*(t, x) = \hat{u}_i^*(\lambda_i)$ for $i = 1,..., N$ is uniquely solvable. Then the trilinear game admits a unique open-loop equilibrium $\hat{u}^*(\lambda_1(\cdot),..., \lambda_N(\cdot))$ which is subgame perfect.

Proof. The Hamiltonians corresponding to a trilinear game are linear in x. This implies that the costate system mentioned above is independent of the initial state value. Moreover, the conditions of Theorem 2.3 are trivially satisfied. ∎

By expressing structural properties of a trilinear game in terms of conditions imposed on the Hamiltonians, namely

$$\left.\frac{\partial^2 H_i}{\partial u_i \partial_x}\right|_{\partial H_i/\partial u_i = 0} = 0 \tag{4.45a}$$

$$\frac{\partial^2 H_i}{\partial x^2} = 0 \tag{4.45b}$$

Dockner *et al.*[68] characterized the slightly more general class of *state-separable* games. Subgame perfectness of open-loop equilibria does, however, not necessarily imply that the state variables are absent from the corresponding Hamiltonian game equilibrium. The following advertising game[60] illustrates this fact.

Example 4.1. Two firms who sell substitutable products influence each other's (and, of course, their own) market share x_i, $i = 1, 2$, by the instantaneous rate of advertising expenditure u_i, $i=1, 2$. The competition between the firms is modeled by the following game:

$$\max_{u_i} \int_0^T (p_i x_i - u_i)\, dt \tag{4.46a}$$

subject to

$$\dot{x}_i = -\beta_i x_i + u_i - c_i u_i^2/2 - k_i x_i u_j$$

$$x_i(0) = x_{i0}; \qquad i=1, 2 \tag{4.46b}$$

$$0 \leqslant x_i, \qquad i=1, 2; \qquad x_1 + x_2 \leqslant 1 \tag{4.46c}$$

$$0 \leqslant u_i \leqslant 1/c_i \tag{4.46d}$$

The parameter β_i denotes the ith firm's decay rate of market share; p_i is the revenue rate. The parabolic advertising effectiveness term $u_i - c_i u_i^2/2$ in condition (4.46b) indicates that advertising is subjected to decreasing returns. We refer to Feichtinger[(69)] for an extension, and a more detailed discussion of this model. For the present exposition, we shall use the restriction

$$\beta_i \geqslant 1/(2c_1) + 1/(2c_2), \qquad i=1, 2 \tag{4.47}$$

in order to ensure the inactivity of condition (4.46c).

The ith player's Hamiltonian is given by

$$H_i = p_i x_i - u_i + \mu_{ii}(-\beta_i x_i + u_i - \tfrac{1}{2} c_i u_i^2 - k_i x_i u_j)$$
$$+ \mu_{ij}(-\beta_j x_j + u_j - \tfrac{1}{2} c_j u_j^2 - k_j x_j u_i)$$

for $i, j = 1, 2$, $j \neq i$. The Hamiltonian game admits the following unique equilibrium:

$$\hat{u}_i^*(x_j, \mu_{ii}, \mu_{ij})$$

$$= \begin{cases} \dfrac{1}{c_i} & \text{if } \Lambda_i > \dfrac{1}{c_i} \\ \Lambda_i := \dfrac{(\mu_{ii} - 1 - \mu_{ij} k_j x_j)}{c_i \mu_{ii}} & \text{if } 0 \leqslant \Lambda_i \leqslant \dfrac{1}{c_i}, \quad i = 1, 2 \\ 0 & \text{otherwise} \end{cases} \tag{4.48}$$

By setting

$$\phi_i^*(t, x_j) = \hat{u}_j^*(x_j, \lambda_{ii}(t), \lambda_{ij}(t)), \qquad i = 1, 2 \tag{4.49}$$

we obtain from conditions (2.31a,b) the following set of differential equations:

$$\begin{aligned} \dot{\lambda}_{ii} = {} & -p_i + \lambda_{ii} \left[\beta_i + k_i \phi_j^*(t, x_j^*) + k_i x_i^* \frac{\partial}{\partial x_i} \phi_j^*(t, x_i^*) \right] \\ & - \lambda_{ij} [1 - c_j \phi_j^*(t, x_i^*)] \frac{\partial}{\partial x_i} \phi_j(t, x_i^*); \qquad \lambda_{ii}(T) = 0 \end{aligned} \tag{4.50a}$$

$$\begin{aligned} \dot{\lambda}_{ij} = {} & \quad + \lambda_{ij} \left[\beta_j + k_j \phi_i^*(t, x_j^*) + k_j x_j^* \frac{\partial}{\partial x_j} \phi_i^*(t, x_j^*) \right] \\ & - \lambda_{ii} [1 - c_i \phi_i^*(t, x_j^*)] \frac{\partial}{\partial x_j} \phi_i^*(t, x_j^*); \qquad \lambda_{ij}(T) = 0 \end{aligned} \tag{4.50b}$$

for $i, j = 1, 2; j \neq i$, and with $x_i^*(\cdot)$, $i = 1, 2$ denoting the unique state trajectory corresponding to solution (4.49).

Since

$$\frac{\partial}{\partial x_j}\phi_i^*(t, x_j^*(t))$$

$$= \begin{cases} \dfrac{-\lambda_{ij}(t)\,k_j}{c_i\lambda_{ii}(t)} & \text{if } 0 < \dfrac{\lambda_{ii}(t)-1-\lambda_{ij}(t)\,k_j x_j^*(t)}{c_i\lambda_{ii}(t)} < \dfrac{1}{c_i} \\ 0 & \text{otherwise} \end{cases} \tag{4.51}$$

the differential equation (4.50b) admits the trivial solution $\lambda_{ij}(t)=0$ for all $t\in[0, T]$. Thus the pair of open-loop decision rules (given by)

$$\phi_i^*(t)= \begin{cases} \dfrac{(\lambda_{ii}(t)-1)}{c_i\lambda_{ii}(t)} & \text{if } \lambda_{ii}(t)\geqslant 1 \\ 0 & \text{otherwise} \end{cases} \qquad i=1, 2 \tag{4.52}$$

qualifies as a subgame perfect equilibrium. ∎

Summarizing the results stated so far, the subgame perfectness of open-loop equilibria occurs for the following reason. After replacement of multipliers by the solutions of the corresponding costate equations, the Hamiltonian maximizing conditions $\partial H_i/\partial u_i=0$ are independent of the state variables, and the initial state value. Games which are characterized by this property will be called *state-redundant*.

Another game, one which is not state-redundant but which also admits only subgame perfect open-loop equilibria, has been investigated by Reinganum.[61] Consider

$$\max_{u_i \in U_i} \int_{t_0}^{T} g_i(t, u_1, \ldots, u_N) \exp(-\xi_i x)\, dt \qquad (4.53a)$$

subject to

$$\dot{x} = f(t, u_1, \ldots, u_N); \qquad x(t_0) = x_0 \qquad (4.53b)$$

where ξ_i, $i = 1, \ldots, N$ is an n-dimensional row vector, and where the functions f and g_i, $i = 1, \ldots, N$, are continuous with respect to time, and continuously differentiable with respect to the remaining arguments.

Theorem 4.9. Suppose that the Hamiltonian game corresponding to system (4.53a,b) admits $\hat{u}^* = (\hat{u}_1^*, \ldots, \hat{u}_N^*)$ as unique equilibrium, where each $\hat{u}_i^*$ may be written as

$$\begin{aligned} \hat{u}_i^* = \hat{u}_i^*(t, \mu_{11} \exp(\xi_1 x), \ldots, \mu_{1n} \exp(\xi_1 x), \ldots, \\ \mu_{N1} \exp(\xi_N x), \ldots, \mu_{Nn} \exp(\xi_N x)) \end{aligned} \qquad (4.54)$$

and where μ_{ij} denotes the jth component of the multiplier μ_i. If the system of differential equations

$$\dot{h}_i = h_i \xi_i f(t, \tilde{u}_1, \ldots, \tilde{u}_N) - g_i(t, \tilde{u}_1, \ldots, \tilde{u}_N); \quad h_i(T) = 0 \qquad (4.55)$$

for $i = 1, \ldots, N$, with

$$\begin{aligned} \tilde{u}_i(t) := \hat{u}_i^*(t, -\xi_{11} h_1(t), \ldots, -\xi_{1n} h_1(t), \ldots, \\ -\xi_{N1} h_N(t), \ldots, -\xi_{Nn} h_N(t)) \end{aligned} \qquad (4.56)$$

is uniquely solvable on $[t_0, T]$, then there exists a subgame perfect, open-loop equilibrium of the *exponential* game (4.53a, b).

Proof. Define (*value*) functions

$$V_i(t, x) := h_i(t) \exp(-\xi_i x); \qquad i = 1,\dots, N \quad (4.57)$$

with $h_i(\cdot)$, $i = 1,\dots, N$, given as the unique solution of equation (4.55). Since the conditions of Theorem 2.4 are satisfied, the N-tuple of open-loop decision rules $(\tilde{u}_1(\cdot),\dots, \tilde{u}_N(\cdot))$ is a subgame perfect equilibrium. ▮

4.2.2. Identifying Perfect Games

The typological connection between the games considered in the previous section may be easily clarified by defining new state variables

$$y_i = \exp(-\xi_i x), \qquad i = 1,\dots, N \qquad (4.58)$$

for the exponential game (4.53a,b). The transformed game is given by

$$\max_{u_i \in U_i} \int_{t_0}^{T} g_i(t, u_1,\dots, u_N)\, y_i\, dt \qquad (4.59a)$$

subject to

$$\dot{y}_i = -\xi_i f(t, u_1,\dots, u_N)\, y_i; \qquad y_i(t_0) = \exp(-\xi_i x_0)$$
$$i = 1,\dots, N \qquad (4.59b)$$

The following extends a result of Mehlmann and Willing.[62]

Theorem 4.10. Let the hypotheses of Theorem 4.9 be satisfied. Then the differential game (4.59a, b) is state-redundant.

Proof. From equations (4.54) and (4.58) it may be shown that the Hamiltonian game corresponding to system (4.59a,b) admits the following unique equilibrium:

$$\hat{u}_i^* = \hat{u}_i^*(t, \eta_{11}, \ldots, \eta_{1n}, \ldots, \eta_{N1}, \ldots, \eta_{Nn}), \qquad i = 1, \ldots, N \tag{4.60}$$

with η_{ij} given by

$$\eta_{ij} = -\sum_{k=1}^{N} \xi_{kj} \mu_{ik} y_k / y_i \tag{4.61}$$

Replace the multipliers μ_{ij} by the costate values $\lambda_{ij}(t)$, with $\lambda_{ij}(\cdot)$, $i, j = 1, \ldots, N$, satisfying the following system of differential equations:

$$\begin{aligned}\dot{\lambda}_{ij} = {} & -\delta_{ij} g_i(t, \bar{u}_1, \ldots, \bar{u}_N) + \lambda_{ij} \xi_j f(t, \bar{u}_1, \ldots, \bar{u}_N) \\ & - \sum_{l \neq i} \left(\frac{\partial g_i(t, \bar{u}_1, \ldots, \bar{u}_N)}{\partial u_l} y_i \right. \\ & \left. - \sum_{k=1}^{N} \lambda_{ik} \xi_k \frac{\partial f(t, \bar{u}_1, \ldots, \bar{u}_N)}{\partial u_l} \right) \\ & \cdot \sum_{m=1}^{N} \sum_{k=1}^{n} \left(\frac{\partial \hat{u}_l^*}{\partial \eta_{mk}} \frac{\partial \eta_{mk}}{\partial y_j} \right) \Bigg|_{t, (\mu_{rs} = \lambda_{rs}(t), y_r = \bar{y}_r(t) \, \forall r, s)} \\ \lambda_{ij}(T) = {} & 0 \end{aligned} \tag{4.62}$$

where the control path $\bar{u}_i(\cdot)$ is defined by

$$\bar{u}_i(t) = \hat{u}_i^* \mid_{t,(\mu_{rs} = \lambda_{rs}(t), y_r = \bar{y}_r(t)\ \forall r,s)} \tag{4.63}$$

and $\bar{y}_i(\cdot)$, $i = 1,\ldots, N$, denotes the unique state trajectory corresponding to the outcome $(\bar{u}_1,\ldots, \bar{u}_N)$. The term δ_{ij} denotes Kronecker's delta, i.e.,

$$\delta_{ij} = \begin{cases} 1 & \text{if } i = j \\ 0 & \text{otherwise} \end{cases}$$

Note that the partial derivative of $\hat{u}_i^*$ with respect to y_j is a linear combination of v_{jr} and v_{sj}, with $r, s \neq j$. Therefore, it can be shown that the $\lambda_{ij}(\cdot)$, $i \neq j$, form a subsystem of differential equations, with the trivial solution $\lambda_{ij}(t) = 0$ for all $t \in [t_0, T]$. Moreover, $\lambda_{ii}(\cdot)$, $i = 1,\ldots, N$ is the unique solution of equation (4.55). The functional form of expression (4.61) combined with the preceding yields the desired property for the differential game (4.59a,b). ∎

A general approach to the identification of games in which open-loop equilibria are necessarily subgame perfect (henceforth called *perfect* games) has been suggested by Fershtman.[63] Let us say that two differential games which admit the same set of open-loop (feedback) equilibria are *open-loop* (*feedback*) *equivalent*. Denote by $\Gamma_{T;x_0}$ a finite horizon differential game starting at the initial state value x_0. In addition, we limit initial state values to those lying in a given set $X_0 \subseteq R^n$. The following result[63] is stated without proof.

Theorem 4.11. Suppose that there exists an initial

state value $\chi_0 \in X_0$ such that for all $x_0 \in X_0$ the differential games $\Gamma_{T;x_0}$ and $\Gamma_{T;\chi_0}$ are open-loop equivalent. Then (each) $\Gamma_{T;x_0}$ is perfect (and *vice versa*).

State transformations are the main tool of proving the perfectness of a given game. Using the diffeomorphisms

$$z_i = y_i/\exp(-\xi_i x_0), \qquad i = 1,..., N$$

and bearing in mind that premultiplication of the ith player's payoff by a constant, say, $\exp(-\xi_i x_0)$ does not change the set of equilibria, Theorem 4.11 with $\chi_0 = 1$ may be applied to prove the perfectness of game (4.59a, b). Feedback equilibria of (4.59a, b) are also equilibria of the exponential game. Since equation (4.58) is (in general) a nonbijective state transformation, the converse does not hold. Both games are, however, open-loop equivalent. Theorem 4.11 therefore applies to the exponential game as well.

Remark 4.3. Fershtman's identification technique does not indicate a method for finding the subgame perfect, open-loop equilibria of a perfect game. This problem is answered by the claim implicitly issued by Mehlmann and Willing[(62)]: any perfect game is either state-redundant or can be transformed to a state-redundant game.

4.3. Qualitatively Solvable Games

In this section, our attention will be focused for the most part upon the qualitative characterization of equilibria. In the majority of cases, one is not able to explicitly derive an equilibrium at the Hamiltonian level. Under the assumption that (for each $i = 1,\ldots, N$) the ith player's Hamiltonian is strictly concave in u_i, and that its maximum with respect to u_i belongs to the interior of U_i, we can capture these situations by considering instead the *Hamiltonian maximizing conditions*

$$H_{iu_i}\left(:= \frac{\partial H_i}{\partial u_i}\right) = 0, \qquad i = 1,\ldots, N \tag{4.64}$$

We begin by introducing the concept of a qualitatively solvable game in a simple, low-dimensional setting. Let the data of a differential game satisfy the following conditions for $i = 1,\ldots, N$:

1. $N = 2;\ 1 \leqslant n \leqslant 2;\ m_i = 1$.
2. U_i is a convex subset of R.
3. $H_i(t, x, u, \mu_i)$ is sufficiently smooth in (x, u), and does not depend explicitly on t.
4. The (necessarily unique) maximum of H_i with respect to u_i belongs to the interior of U_i.
5. $H^0_{iu_iu_i} := (H_{iu_iu_i} \mid_{H_{iu_i} = 0}) < 0$, where $H_{iu_iu_i} := \partial^2 H_i / (\partial u_i)^2$.

The unique maximum $\hat{u}_i$ of H_i is now implicitly given as a function of x, u_{-i}, and μ_i, i.e.,

$$\hat{u}_i = \hat{u}_i(x, u_{-i}, \mu_i) \tag{4.65}$$

From

$$dH_{iu_i} = H_{iu_ix}\, dx + \sum_{j=1}^{2} H_{iu_iu_j}\, du_j + f_{u_i}\, d\mu_i \tag{4.66}$$

we obtain

$$\frac{\partial \hat{u}_i}{\partial x} = -\frac{H^0_{i_{u_i x}}}{H^0_{i_{u_i u_i}}}, \quad \frac{\partial \hat{u}_i}{\partial u_j} = -\frac{H^0_{i_{u_i u_j}}}{H^0_{i_{u_i u_i}}}, \quad \frac{\partial \hat{u}_i}{\partial \mu_i} = -\frac{f^0_{u_i}}{H^0_{i_{u_i u_i}}} \tag{4.67}$$

where the exponent ^{0} indicates the evaluation at $H_{i_{u_i}} = 0$.

We shall say that a differential game given by (1)–(5) is *qualitatively solvable*, if (at least one) of its (subgame perfect) equilibria may be analyzed by phase diagrams. In what follows, we identify two classes* of qualitatively solvable games.

4.3.1. Phase Diagram Analysis of Perfect Games

Under the additional assumption

$$6. \quad \Lambda^0 := H^0_{1_{u_1 u_1}} H^0_{2_{u_2 u_2}} - H^0_{1_{u_1 u_2}} H^0_{2_{u_2 u_1}} > 0 \tag{4.68}$$

the unique equilibrium $\hat{u}^* = (\hat{u}_1^*, \hat{u}_2^*)$ of the Hamiltonian game is implicitly given as a function of x, μ_1, and μ_2. Moreover, the following relations hold:

$$\frac{\partial \hat{u}_i^*}{\partial x_l} = -\frac{1}{\Lambda^0} \det \begin{vmatrix} H^0_{i_{u_i x_l}} & H^0_{i_{u_i u_j}} \\ H^0_{j_{u_j x_l}} & H^0_{j_{u_j u_j}} \end{vmatrix}; \qquad \frac{\partial \hat{u}_i^*}{\partial \mu_{il}} = -\frac{f^0_{l_{u_i}} H^0_{j_{u_j u_j}}}{\Lambda^0};$$

$$\frac{\partial \hat{u}_i^*}{\partial \mu_{jl}} = \frac{f^0_{l_{u_j}} H^0_{i_{u_i u_j}}}{\Lambda^0} \tag{4.69}$$

* In Exercise 5.5, a qualitatively solvable game is presented which is neither perfect nor symmetric.

for $i, j = 1, 2, i \neq j$. If the state is a scalar variable, delete the index l. Otherwise x_l, f_l, and μ_{il} denote the lth components of x, f, and μ_i, respectively; $f_{l_{u_i}}$ denotes the partial derivative of f_l with respect to u_i.

The approach to follow is based on Dockner *et al.*[68] For $n = 2$, impose one of the following additional restrictions on the game's structure:

7.
$$f(x, u) = (f_1(x_1, u_1), f_2(x_2, u_2))'$$
$$L_{i_{u_i x_j}} = 0; \qquad L_{i_{x_i x_j}} = 0$$
$$S_i(T, x) = s_i x_i + \phi_i(T, x_j)$$

7′.
$$f(x, u) = (f_1(x_1, u), f_2(x_2, u))'; \qquad f_{i_{u_i}} \neq 0$$
$$L_i(x, u) = L_i(x_i, u)$$
$$S_i(T, x) = s_i x_i$$

Theorem 4.12. Suppose that

(a) $$H^0_{i_{u_i x_i}} = 0$$
(b) $$H_{i_{x_i x_i}} = 0$$
(c) the system of equations

$$s_i = -F_{i_{u_i}}/f_{i_{u_i}} \tag{4.70}$$

is uniquely solvable in u_1, u_2.

Then a subgame-perfect, open-loop equilibrium of the game under consideration is determined by (the solution of) the following system of differential equations:

$$\dot{u}_i = \Phi_i(u_1, u_2)$$

$$= \frac{\det \begin{vmatrix} f_{iu_i}F_{ix_i} - f_{ix_i}F_{iu_i} & F_{iu_iu_j} - f_{iu_iu_j}F_{iu_i}/f_{iu_i} \\ f_{ju_j}F_{jx_j} - f_{jx_j}F_{ju_j} & F_{ju_ju_j} - f_{ju_ju_j}F_{ju_j}/f_{ju_j} \end{vmatrix}}{\det \begin{vmatrix} F_{1u_1u_1} - f_{1u_1u_1}F_{1u_1}/f_{1u_1} & F_{1u_1u_2} - f_{1u_1u_2}F_{1u_1}/f_{1u_1} \\ F_{2u_2u_1} - f_{2u_2u_1}F_{2u_2}/f_{2u_2} & F_{2u_2u_2} - f_{2u_2u_2}F_{2u_2}/f_{2u_2} \end{vmatrix}} \tag{4.71a}$$

$$u_i(T) = u_{iT}; \qquad i, j = 1, 2, \qquad i \neq j \tag{4.71b}$$

with u_{iT}, $i = 1, 2$ denoting the solution of equation (4.70).

Proof. Let $n = 2$. If either restriction (7) or (7′) holds, then the ith player's Hamiltonian

$$L_i(x, u) + \mu_{i1} f_1(x, u) + \mu_{i2} f_2(x, u)$$

may be replaced by

$$L_i(x, u) + \mu_{ii} f_i(x, u)$$

(The costate corresponding to the other multiplier is either irrelevant for the ith player's maximization procedure, or will vanish on $[t_0, T]$.) The assumptions (7), (7′), and (a) imply that $\partial \hat{u}_i^* / \partial x_l = 0$ for $i, l = 1, 2$.

From conditions (4.64) and $f_{iu_i} \neq 0$ we may derive

$$\mu_{ii} = -\frac{L_{iu_i}}{f_{iu_i}} \tag{4.72}$$

Quantity $H^0_{iu_ix_i}$ is then given by

$$L_{iu_ix_i} - f_{iu_ix_i} L_{iu_i}/f_{iu_i} \tag{4.73}$$

We claim that F_{iu_i}/f_{iu_i} is independent of x_i, if $H^0_{iu_ix_i}=0$. To see this, assume first that $f_{iu_ix_i}=0$, and observe [from expression (4.73)] that $F_{iu_ix_i}$ necessarily vanishes. If $f_{iu_ix_i}\neq 0$, the following equality holds:

$$\frac{F_{iu_ix_i}}{f_{iu_ix_i}}=\frac{F_{iu_i}}{f_{iu_i}} \tag{4.74}$$

From

$$\frac{\partial}{\partial x_i}\left(\frac{F_{iu_i}}{f_{iu_i}}\right)=\frac{F_{iu_ix_i}}{f_{iu_i}}-\frac{F_{iu_i}}{f_{iu_i}}\frac{f_{iu_ix_i}}{f_{iu_i}}$$

and equality (4.74) the claim is verified.

Assume that μ_{ii} satisfies the costate equation

$$\dot{\mu}_{ii}=-H^0_{ix_i}-H^0_{iu_j}\frac{\partial\hat{u}_j^*}{\partial x_i};\qquad \mu_{ii}(T)=s_i$$

By taking the derivative of conditions (4.64) with respect to time, one obtains

$$H^0_{iu_iu_i}\dot{u}_i+H^0_{iu_iu_j}\dot{u}_j+H^0_{iu_i\mu_{ii}}\dot{\mu}_{ii}+H^0_{iu_ix_i}\dot{x}_i+H^0_{iu_ix_j}\dot{x}_j=0 \tag{4.75}$$

The left-hand side of equation (4.75) reduces to

$$H^0_{iu_iu_i}\dot{u}_i+H^0_{iu_iu_j}\dot{u}_j-f^0_{iu_i}H^0_{ix_i} \tag{4.76}$$

From relations (4.72), (4.76), and assumption (c), we derive the system of differential equations (4.71a,b). Due to assumptions (7), (7′), (a) and (b), this system is independent of the state variables. A solution $(u_1^*(\cdot),$

$u_2^*(\cdot)$) of equations (4.71a,b) is necessarily a subgame perfect, open-loop equilibrium. (Why?) In Exercise 4.5 you are asked to complete the proof for $n=1$. ∎

Setting $\dot{u}_i=0$, $i=1, 2$, we obtain the *isoclines* of system (4.71a) in the form

$$\Phi_i(u_1, u_2)=0; \qquad i=1, 2 \tag{4.77}$$

An intersection of these curves is called a *stationary point*. The behavior of solution paths near a stationary point, say, (u_1^s, u_2^s), depends on the eigenvalues ξ_1, ξ_2 of the *Jacobian* matrix

$$J^s=\begin{bmatrix} \Phi^s_{1_{u_1}} & \Phi^s_{1_{u_2}} \\ \Phi^s_{2_{u_1}} & \Phi^s_{2_{u_2}} \end{bmatrix} \tag{4.78}$$

where $\Phi^s_{i_{u_j}} := (\partial\Phi_i(u_1, u_2)/\partial u_j)\,|_{u_1=u_1^s;u_2=u_2^s}$. The eigenvalues satisfy

$$\xi_1\xi_2=\det J^s := \Phi^s_{1_{u_1}}\Phi^s_{2_{u_2}} - \Phi^s_{1_{u_2}}\Phi^s_{2_{u_1}} \tag{4.79a}$$

$$\xi_1+\xi_2=\text{trace } J^s := \Phi^s_{1_{u_1}} + \Phi^s_{2_{u_2}} \tag{4.79b}$$

It is now possible to distinguish different types of stationary points (see Table 1).

TABLE 1. Types of Stationary Points

(u_1^s, u_2^s)	Jacobian J^s
Saddlepoint	$\det J^s<0$
Stable node	$0<\det J^s\leqslant(\text{trace } J^s)^2/4$; $\text{trace } J^s<0$
Unstable node	$0<\det J^s\leqslant(\text{trace } J^s)^2/4$; $\text{trace } J^s>0$
Stable focus	$\det J^s>(\text{trace } J^s)^2/4$; $\text{trace } J^s<0$
Unstable focus	$\det J^s>(\text{trace } J^s)^2/4$; $\text{trace } J^s>0$

Example 4.2. Again let us consider Faust's game in Section 1.2.1. Applying Theorem 4.12 we can see that the unique subgame perfect, open-loop equilibrium is determined by

$$\dot{u}_1 = \frac{c_1}{2}\left(u_1^2 - \frac{d_2}{d_1} u_2\right) \tag{4.80a}$$

$$\dot{u}_2 = \frac{c_2}{2} u_2^2 - \frac{c_1 d_2}{2d_1} u_2 + \left(\frac{c_1}{2} - \frac{c_2 g_1}{2g_2}\right) u_1^2 + \frac{c_2 g_1}{2g_2} \bar{u} u_1 \tag{4.80b}$$

$$u_1(T) = u_2(T) = \frac{Vc_1}{2d_1} \tag{4.80c}$$

The u_1-isocline is a parabola, while the u_2-isocline is an arbitrary conic section. It can be easily seen that the origin of the (u_1, u_2)-plane is either a stable node or a stable focus. This follows directly from the Jacobian

$$\begin{bmatrix} 0 & -c_1 d_2/(2d_1) \\ c_2 g_1 \bar{u}/(2g_2) & -c_1 d_2/(2d_1) \end{bmatrix} \tag{4.81}$$

There exist also other stationary points which satisfy the following equations:

$$u_1^3 - \frac{g_1 d_2^2}{g_2 d_1^2}(u_1 - \bar{u}) = 0 \tag{4.82a}$$

$$u_1^2 - \frac{d_2}{d_1} u_2 = 0 \tag{4.82b}$$

The cubic equation (4.82a) admits three real solutions, if

$$\frac{d_2}{d_1}\left(\frac{g_1}{3g_2}\right)^{1/2} > \frac{3}{2}\bar{u} \tag{4.83}$$

From the elementary theory of cubic equations, we have

$$0 < u_1^{\bar{s}} < \frac{d_2}{d_1}\left(\frac{g_1}{3g_2}\right)^{1/2} < u_1^{\hat{s}} \tag{4.84a}$$

and, therefore, from equation (4.82b)

$$0 < u_2^{\bar{s}} < \frac{d_2 g_1}{3d_1 g_2} < u_2^{\hat{s}} \tag{4.84b}$$

for the two stationary points $(u_1^{\bar{s}}, u_2^{\bar{s}})$ and $(u_1^{\hat{s}}, u_2^{\hat{s}})$ located in the positive orthant of the (u_1, u_2)-plane. These two points coincide if the inequality sign in relation (4.83) is replaced by equality. The art of how to set up a phase diagram (for this and other games) will be illustrated in greater detail in the following chapter. ∎

Remark 4.4. In perfect games, an outcome corresponding to a feedback equilibrium is (necessarily) independent of the initial state value x_0. Thus, the technique of phase diagram analysis is not limited to the case of open-loop, subgame perfect equilibria.

4.3.2. Symmetric Games with a Single State Variable

Replace assumption (1) by

1. $n = 1$; $m_i = 1$.

and assume that the differential game is symmetric with respect to the state and the control variables, i.e.,

$$H_{i_x} = H_{k_x}(=: H_x); \qquad H_{i_{u_i}} = H_{k_{u_k}}(=: H_{u_\bullet});$$
$$\sum_{j \neq i} H_{i_{u_j}} = \sum_{l \neq k} H_{k_{u_l}}(=: H_{u_{\bar{\bullet}}}) \tag{4.85}$$

for $k, i = 1,..., N$, $k \neq i$. Clemhout and Wan[70] seek to determine a time invariant, symmetric feedback equilibrium $u^*(x) = (u_\bullet^*(x),..., u_\bullet^*(x))$. By taking the derivative of conditions (4.64) with respect to time, one obtains

$$\sum_{j=1}^{N} H^0_{i_{u_i u_j}} \dot{u}_j + f^0_{u_i} \dot{\mu}_i + H^0_{i_{u_i x}} f^0 = 0 \tag{4.86}$$

where $\mu_i(\cdot)$ satisfies the costate equation

$$\dot{\mu}_i = -H^0_{i_{x_i}} - \sum_{j \neq i} H^0_{i_{u_j}} \frac{du_\bullet^*}{dx} \tag{4.87}$$

Assume that $f_{u_i} \neq 0$ for $i = 1,..., N$. Then the exponent ^{0} attached to the Hamiltonian derivatives indicates replacement of μ_i by $-L_{i_{u_i}}/f_{u_i}$.

In view of the postulated symmetry and time-invariancy, we have

$$u_\bullet^{*\prime}(x) := \frac{du_\bullet^*}{dx} = \frac{\dot{u}_\bullet}{f^0} \tag{4.88}$$

where $u_\bullet(\cdot)$ denotes any player's control path. From equations (4.87) and (4.88) it can be shown that

$$\dot{u}_\bullet = f \frac{H^0_x f_{u_\bullet} - H^0_{u_\bullet x} f}{(H^0_{u_\bullet u_\bullet} + H^0_{u_\bullet u_{\bar{\bullet}}}) f - H^0_{u_{\bar{\bullet}}} f_{u_\bullet}} \tag{4.89}$$

Consider the autonomous system of equations (4.89) and

$$\dot{x} = f(t, u_\bullet, \ldots, u_\bullet) \tag{4.90}$$

All points on the isocline $f = 0$ are stationary points. Since the corresponding Jacobian matrices are singular, the linear system approximation of equations (4.89) and (4.90) is not *structurally stable.**

In order to find a time-dependent, symmetric equilibrium, we take the derivative of conditions (4.64) with respect to x, and obtain

$$\frac{\partial \hat{u}^*_\bullet}{\partial x} = -\frac{H^0_{u_\bullet x}}{H^0_{u_\bullet u_\bullet} + H^0_{u_\bullet u_\bullet^-}} \tag{4.91}$$

Replace the total derivative $du^*_\bullet/dx$ in equation (4.87) by relation (4.91). Then we find that equation (4.90) and

$$\dot{u}_\bullet = \frac{H^0_x f_{u_\bullet} - H^0_{u_\bullet x} f}{H^0_{u_\bullet u_\bullet} + H^0_{u_\bullet u_\bullet^-}} - \frac{H^0_{u_\bullet x} H^0_{u_\bullet^-} f_{u_\bullet}}{(H^0_{u_\bullet u_\bullet} + H^0_{u_\bullet u_\bullet^-})^2} \tag{4.92}$$

is the corresponding autonomous system.

Remark 4.5. In the case that $H_i(t, x, u, \mu_i) := e^{-rt}\tilde{L}_i(x, u) + \mu_i f(x, u)$ we may obtain an autonomous problem by replacing the multipliers μ_i by $v_i e^{-rt}$, and define the *current value* Hamiltonians

$$\tilde{H}_i := e^{rt} H_i = \tilde{L}_i + v_i f \tag{4.93}$$

* A qualitative characterization of the equilibrium outcome is nevertheless possible. See Section 5.4.2.

Note that the new costate equations are given by

$$\dot{v}_i = r v_i + e^{rt} \dot{\mu}_i \tag{4.94}$$

Then, the differential equation (4.92) must be rewritten in the following way:

$$\dot{u}_{\bullet} = \frac{r\tilde{L}_{u_\bullet} + \tilde{H}^0_x f_{u_\bullet} - \tilde{H}^0_{u_\bullet x} f}{\tilde{H}^0_{u_\bullet u_\bullet} + \tilde{H}^0_{u_\bullet u_{\bar{\bullet}}}} - \frac{\tilde{H}^0_{u_\bullet x} \tilde{H}^0_{u_{\bar{\bullet}}} f_{u_\bullet}}{(\tilde{H}^0_{u_\bullet u_\bullet} + \tilde{H}^0_{u_\bullet u_{\bar{\bullet}}})^2} \tag{4.95}$$

where the exponent ^{0} attached to the (current value) Hamiltonian derivatives indicates replacement of v_i by $-\tilde{L}_{u_\bullet}/f_{u_\bullet}$.

Exercises

4.1. Consider the following (two-person) differential game:

$$\max_{u_1 \in R^{m_1}} \frac{1}{2} \left\{ \int_{t_0}^{T} \left[x' Q_1(t)\, x + \sum_{j=1}^{2} u_j' S_{1j}(t)\, u_j \right] dt + x'(T)\, Q_1^{(T)} x(T) \right\}$$

$$\max_{u_2 \in R^{m_2}} \frac{1}{2} \left\{ \int_{t_0}^{T} \left[x' Q_2(t)\, x + 2u_1' W(t)\, u_2 + \sum_{j=1}^{2} u_j' S_{2j}(t)\, u_j \right] dt + x'(T)\, Q_2^{(T)} x(T) \right\}$$

subject to

$$\dot{x} = A(t)\, x + \sum_{i=1}^{2} B_i(t)\, u_i; \qquad x(t_0) = x_0 (\in R^n)$$

(a) Generalize the results of Section 4.1 to this class of linear-quadratic games.

(b) Obtain conditions for the existence of a unique memoryless equilibrium $((\hat{\psi}_1(t), \hat{\psi}_2(t, u_1))$.

(c) Deduce affine equilibria adapted to the extensive situation (3.48).

4.2. Consider the following differential game[(62)]:

$$\max_{u_1} \left\{ J_1 = \int_0^1 (4x - x^2 u_1^2)\, dt - 4x(1) \right\}$$

$$\max_{u_2} \left\{ J_2 = \int_0^1 [x^2(3t^2 - u_2^2) - 2x]\, dt + 2x(1) \right\}$$

subject to

$$\dot{x} = -x^2(u_1 + u_2); \qquad x(0) = 1$$

Show that this game is not state separable, but state redundant.
(*Hint*: Solve the corresponding costate equations.)

4.3. Identify the class of games for which open-loop equilibria are Pareto-efficient outcomes.

4.4. Characterize the class of games which admit subgame perfect, memoryless equilibria [adapted, say, to the extensive situation (3.48)].
[*Hint*: Utilize the term $\partial \hat{u}_2 / \partial u_1$ from system (4.67) in order to deduce the leader's Hamiltonian maximizing condition.]

4.5. Complete the proof of Theorem 4.12 for $n = 1$.

4.6. Generalize Theorem 4.12 to the case of subgame-perfect memoryless equilibria (treated in Exercise 4.4).

4.7. Recall the Eskimoean fishery game of Example 3.4. Deduce (equilibrium) outcomes corresponding to the extensive situations (2.50) and (3.48) by utilizing Theorem 4.12 and Exercise 4.6.

5
Selected Applications

Call it infantile *vendetta*
on life's deeply serious aim—
you will know existence better
once you understand our game.

Christian Morgenstern*

The purpose of this chapter is to design different aspects of dynamic conflict by means of differential game models. We limit our field of view to the following areas: literary analysis, theory of the firm(s), research and development, and management of renewable resources. No attempts will be made to survey the literature in each field.*

5.1. Faust—The Game

> Mathematicians are like Frenchmen:
> whatever you say to them
> they translate into their own language
> and forthwith it is something entirely different.
>
> J. W. von Goethe

The interface between game theory and literature is a neglected but fascinating topic. In von Neumann and Morgenstern,[1] an episode from Conan-Doyle's "Adventures of Sherlock Holmes" is considered and solved by means of a zero-sum matrix game. Brams[71] presents a "play-by-play" analysis of Old Testament stories. Interpretations of theatrical works as normal form (matrix) games and as metagames are given in Lalu[72] (Shakespeare's "Richard iii"), Rapoport[73] and Teodorescu-Brînzeu[74] (Shakespeare's "Othello"), Howard[29]

* A selected bibliography is given at the end of this book.

(Pinter's "The Caretaker"), and Vorobyev.[75] In the present section, we deal with the only serious attempt[18,19] at literary analysis using the intertemporal decision framework of differential games. The model offered in Section 1.2.1 will serve as a mathematical description of both Goethe's drama and the original Faust legend. To find textual confirmation with both versions, we shall limit Goethe's wager to the traditional twenty-four-year horizon after which—according to the old legend—the compact expires.

5.1.1. First Scenario—Goethe's Play

In order to acquire knowledge and power Faust has succumbed to the blandishments of the devil. Let us consider the following scenario:

- (α) The compact's maximal duration is $T = 24$ years.
- (β) At each instant t, Mephisto acts before Faust: $\mathscr{I}_1(t) = \{x(t)\}$; $\mathscr{I}_2(t) = \{x(t), u_1(t)\}$.
- (γ) $c_1 = c_2 = 1$.
- (δ) Mephisto is heavily disturbed by Faust's striving activity: $d_2 = 16 d_1$.
- (ε) Faust gives preference to utility derived from the devil's seduction: $g_1 = 2 g_2$.
- (ζ) Faust's level of satisfaction is comparatively low: $\bar{u} = 4$.

Contrary to Example 4.2, we will derive a subgame perfect (memoryless) equilibrium adapted to the situation

(β) of hierarchical play. A metagame equilibrium of ${}^2\Xi$ is given by*

$$(u_1^{\mathrm{b}}, \rho_2^{\mathrm{b}}); \qquad u_1^{\mathrm{b}} = \frac{c_1(V+\mu_{11}) - d_2 + c_2\mu_{22}(1-x_2)(1-x_1)^{-1}}{2d_1}$$

$$\rho_2^{\mathrm{b}}(u_1) = u_1 + \frac{\mu_{22}c_2}{2g_2} \tag{5.1}$$

Straightforward application of Theorems 3.3 and 3.4 leads to the following hierarchical equilibrium:

$$\hat{\phi}_1(t) = \frac{c_1(V+\lambda_{11}) - d_2}{2d_1} \tag{5.2a}$$

$$\hat{\phi}_2(t, u_1) = u_1 + \frac{\lambda_{22}c_2}{2g_2} \tag{5.2b}$$

where $\lambda_{ii}(\cdot)$, $i = 1, 2$, the players' costate functions with respect to their own belief about the timing of the "supreme Moment," are given by equations (3.52a,b).

The outcome $(\hat{u}_1(\cdot), \hat{u}_2(\cdot))$ corresponding to equations (5.2a,b) is determined by the following autonomous system of differential equations:

$$\dot{u}_1 = \frac{c_1}{2}\left(u_1^2 - \frac{d_2}{d_1}u_2\right) \tag{4.80a}$$

$$\dot{u}_2 = \frac{c_2}{2}u_2^2 - \frac{c_1 d_2}{2d_1}u_2 + \left(\frac{c_1}{2} - \frac{c_2 g_1}{2g_2}\right)u_1^2 + \frac{c_2 g_1}{2g_2}\bar{u}u_1 \tag{4.80b}$$

$$u_1(T) = u_2(T) = \frac{Vc_1 - d_2}{2d_1} \tag{4.80d}$$

* See Example 2.2.

The reader may use the general approach suggested in Exercise 4.6 to derive this system. Simple differentiation of equations (5.2a,b) with respect to time will do the job as well. Note that the phase diagram for system (4.80a,b,d) coincides with the phase plane discussed in Example 4.2. The terminal conditions are, however, distinct.

We desperately need an unstable stationary point in the interior of the positive orthant. Otherwise, the (family of unique) solutions of equations (4.80a,b), one passing through each admissible terminal point (4.80d) (for finite values of $V \geqslant d_2/c_1$), would violate the control constraints $0 \leqslant u_i$. The Jacobian of (u_1^s, u_2^s), for $s = \bar{s}$ and $s = \hat{s}$, is given by

$$J^s = \begin{bmatrix} c_1 u_1^s & -c_1 d_2/(2d_1) \\ c_1 u_1^s - c_2 g_1(2u_1^s - \bar{u})/(2g_2) & c_2 u_2^s - c_1 d_2/(2d_1) \end{bmatrix} \tag{5.3}$$

From equations (4.82a,b) we have

$$\det J^s = \frac{c_1 c_2 d_2 g_1}{2d_1 g_2}\left(u_1^s - \frac{3}{2}\bar{u}\right) \tag{5.4}$$

The precise nature of (0, 0), $(u_1^{\bar{s}}, u_2^{\bar{s}})$, and $(u_1^{\hat{s}}, u_2^{\hat{s}})$ is now given as follows:

(0, 0)	stable focus
$(u_1^{\bar{s}}, u_2^{\bar{s}}) \approx (4.14, 1.07)$	saddlepoint
$(u_1^{\hat{s}}, u_2^{\hat{s}}) \approx (20.27, 25.69)$	unstable node

As shown in Figure 1, both players start their game in the neighborhood of $(u_1^{\hat{s}}, u_2^{\hat{s}})$. We have indicated some

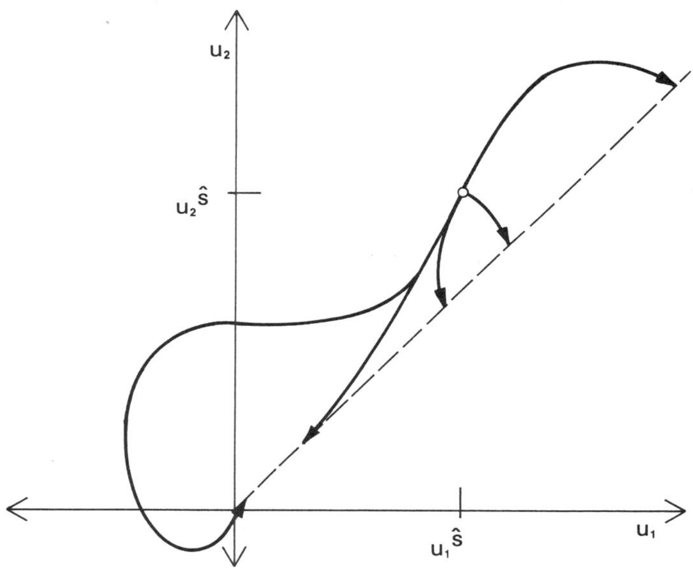

FIGURE 1. The equilibrium solution to Goethe's "Faust."

solution paths which—after spending most of their time* in the vicinity of $(u_1^{\hat{s}}, u_2^{\hat{s}})$—diverge away from the unstable node as t increases, and satisfy the terminal conditions (for the case of a high, medium, moderate, small, and negligible value of $V-d_2/c_1$). All but one of the solution curves are tangent to a line through $(u_1^{\hat{s}}, u_2^{\hat{s}})$ with the same direction as the eigenvector corresponding to the smaller eigenvalue $(\xi_1 \approx 7.5)$ of $J^{\hat{s}}$. The remaining solution (the second curve from above) is tangent to the other eigenvector.

Although Faust gives preference to utility derived

* Approximately 23.5 years.

from the devil's seduction, his equilibrium reaction (5.2b) is to exceed Mephisto's machinations u_1. In the case that Mephisto's temptations have a negative influence on Faust's payoff, i.e., $(u_1 \gg \bar{u})$, Faust will tend to lose the wager as soon as possible. In terms of our expectation model formulation, this means that $x_2(24)$—Faust's subjective probability that the "supreme Moment" will occur—will be made as large as possible under the restriction of avoiding an excessive negative effect on Faust's payoff.

The vicious circle can now be closed. Let us assume that Mephisto has the ability to predict* the strategy choice of Faust. Being heavily disturbed by Faust's level of striving activity, he is forced to reach the end of the game by exaggerated seducement (which will be reduced during the last stage of the compact if and only if the value of Faust's soul is smaller than $3d_2$). But this is exactly the situation in Goethe's "Faust." The "supreme Moment" has been (finally) reached, and the wager seems to have been won by Mephisto. By his will to strive, however, Faust('s immortal soul) is to be saved from eternal damnation.

5.1.2. Second Scenario—The Original Source

Let us consider the following scenario:

(α) The compact's maximal duration is $T = 24$ years.

* Compare the paradoxon of omniscience in Brams.[76] Is Mephisto a "superior being"?

(β) At each instant t, Mephisto acts before Faust: $\mathscr{I}_1(t) = \{x(t)\}$; $\mathscr{I}_2(t) = \{x(t), u_1(t)\}$.

(γ) $c_1 = c_2 = 1$.

(δ) Mephisto is heavily disturbed by Faust's striving activity: $d_2 = 16d_1$.

(ε) Faust gives preference to utility derived from his will to strive: $4g_1 = 3g_2$.

(ζ) Faust's level of satisfaction is comparatively low: $\bar{u} = 4$.

The precise nature of (0, 0), $(u_1^{\bar{s}}, u_2^{\bar{s}})$ and $(u_1^{\hat{s}}, u_2^{\hat{s}})$ is now given as follows:

$(0, 0)$	stable focus
$(u_1^{\bar{s}}, u_2^{\bar{s}}) \approx (4.46, 1.24)$	saddlepoint
$(u_1^{\hat{s}}, u_2^{\hat{s}}) \approx (11.07, 7.66)$	unstable focus

Although Faust gives preference to utility derived from his striving activity, his equilibrium reaction (5.2b) is below Mephisto's level of seduction u_1. Figure 2 and, in particular, the nontrivial qualitative behavior of the second solution curve from below indicates where the tragedy of this scenario lies.

Mephisto provides Faust with more than he wants, but always cheated of the supreme success. In pursuing the devil's pleasures Faust neglects his will to strive. As the twenty-four years draw to their end, we observe a monotonic decline in Mephisto's rate of seduction, while Faust, for the only time before the end, does despair by increasing his striving activity (or repentance). But in awareness of his failure, he ultimately resigns himself to his fate.

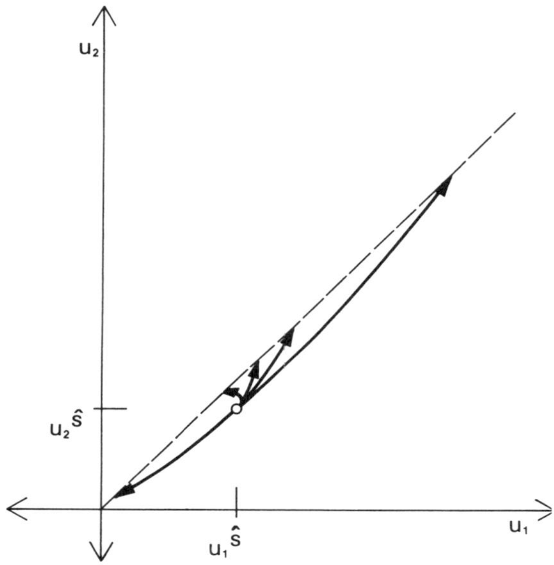

FIGURE 2. The equilibrium solution to the original Faust legend.

This oscillating behavior throughout the last stage of the game is not consistent with Goethe's "Faust." But it is precisely the attitude of the original Faust legend. The "supreme Moment" has not been achieved. It is Faust's low level of striving activity that finally tips the balance in favor of his doom, even though, in legalistic terms, he may have won his bet with Mephisto.

5.2. The Dynamics of Oligopoly

Time only knows the price we have to pay
W. H. Auden

The classic Cournot model of duopoly assumes in its

simplest form that two firms (selling water from a well) face a linear demand curve for their homogeneous product. In Simaan and Takayama's[22] dynamic version* of Cournot's "game"

$$\max_{u_i \geqslant 0} \left\{ J_i = \int_0^T e^{-r_i t} \left[x u_i - c_i u_i - \frac{1}{2} \alpha_i u_i^2 \right] dt \right\} \quad (1.15)$$

subject to

$$\dot{x} = k[a - b(u_1 + u_2) - x]; \qquad x(0) = x_0 \quad (1.16)$$

and

$$x(t) \geqslant 0 \qquad \text{for all } t \in [0, T] \quad (1.17)$$

the change in price, $\dot{x}(t)$, is determined by the difference between the current market price, $x(t)$, and the price given by the (inverse) linear demand

$$\tilde{x}(t) = a - b[u_1(t) + u_2(t)]; \qquad a, b > 0 \quad (1.19)$$

Fershtman and Kamien[78] deal with a symmetric, infinite horizon variant of this game. By interpreting the relaxation constant k as a "speed of adjustment" term, they concentrate on the asymptotic properties (as price adjusts instantaneously) of dynamic solutions. A sequel paper[79] is devoted to the study of the finite horizon duopoly. The authors solve the game by using the value function approach (see Theorem 2.4). In the present sec-

* Because of its historical interest we refer also to Evans's[77] model for a dynamic monopoly.

tion, we apply the approach developed in Section 4.1 to generalize their results to the case of oligopoly.

5.2.1. The Finite Horizon Oligopoly

The (linear-quadratic) game to be solved is given by:

$$\max_{u_i \geqslant 0} \left\{ J_i = \int_0^T e^{-rt} \left[xu_i - cu_i - \frac{1}{2} u_i^2 \right] dt \right\}, \qquad i = 1, \ldots, N \quad (5.5a)$$

subject to

$$\dot{x} = k[a - 2b(u_1 + u_2 + \cdots + u_N)/N - x]; \qquad x(0) = x_0 \quad (5.5b)$$

and

$$x(t) \geqslant 0 \qquad \text{for all } t \in [0, T] \quad (5.5c)$$

Note that the price indicated by the inverse demand

$$\tilde{x}(t) = a - 2b[u_1(t) + u_2(t) + \cdots + u_N(t)]/N; \qquad a > c > 0, \qquad b > 0$$

ensures that each firm's part of the market in a symmetric situation of static oligopoly remains constant as a function of N (see Shubik[(80)]).

Contrary to the linear-quadratic games considered in Section 4.1, the finite-horizon oligopoly game is a constrained N-person game, and has (bi)linear payoff terms.

Nevertheless, we can use much the same methods as in Section 4.1 to derive a subgame perfect feedback equilibrium of this game.

Maximizing the current value Hamiltonians

$$\tilde{H}_i = xu_i - cu_i - u_i^2/2 + v_i k[a - 2b(u_1 + \cdots + u_N)/N - x] \qquad (5.6)$$

with respect to $u_i \geqslant 0$, we get the following Hamiltonian equilibrium:

$$\hat{u}_i(v_i, x) = \begin{cases} x - c - 2bkv_i/N & \text{if} \quad v_i \leqslant \dfrac{x-c}{2bk} \\ 0 & \text{otherwise} \end{cases} \qquad i = 1, \ldots, N \quad (5.7)$$

Substituting

$$v_i = P_i x + v_i; \qquad i = 1, \ldots, N$$

into expression (5.6), we obtain the N-tuple of feedback strategies

$$\psi_i^*(t, x) = \begin{cases} \left(1 - \dfrac{2bkP_i(t)}{N}\right) x - c - \dfrac{2bkv_i(t)}{N} & \text{if } x \geqslant \bar{x}_i(t) \\ 0 & \text{otherwise} \end{cases} \qquad i = 1, \ldots, N \quad (5.8)$$

where

$$\bar{x}_i(t) = \frac{c + 2bkv_i(t)/N}{1 - 2bkP_i(t)/N} \qquad (5.9)$$

Under the assumption that the critical (price level) functions $\bar{x}_i(\cdot)$ are nonnegative, the state constraint $x \geqslant 0$ is not binding over $[0, T]$. The costate equations are then given by

$$\dot{\lambda}_i = \frac{d}{dt}(P_i x^* + v_i) = (r+k)(P_i x^* + v_i) - \psi_i^*(t, x^*) + \frac{2bk}{N}(P_i x^* + v_i) \sum_{j \neq i} \frac{\partial \psi_j^*(t, x^*)}{\partial x} \tag{5.10}$$

$$\lambda_i(T) = P_i(T)\, x^*(T) + v_i(T) = 0,$$

where $x^*(\cdot)$ denotes the state trajectory corresponding to strategies (5.8).

Consider the case of a symmetric solution. From relations (5.8) and (5.10) we may derive the following differential equations for $P_\bullet(\cdot)$ and $v_\bullet(\cdot)$ [which hold, however, in the interior of the region $x \geqslant 0$, $u_\bullet(\cdot) \geqslant 0$ only]:

$$\dot{P}_\bullet = -\frac{4b^2k^2(N+1)}{N^2} P_\bullet^2 + \left(2k + r + \frac{2bk(N+2)}{N}\right) P_\bullet - 1; \qquad P_\bullet(T) = 0 \tag{5.11a}$$

$$\dot{v}_\bullet = c - (ka + 2bkc)\, P_\bullet + \left(-\frac{4b^2k^2(N+1)}{N^2} P_\bullet + r + \frac{(4b+N)\,k}{N}\right) v_\bullet; \qquad v_\bullet(T) = 0 \tag{5.11b}$$

Solving system (5.11a,b) and

$$\dot{x}^* = k[a - 2b\psi_\bullet^*(t, x^*) - x^*]; \qquad (5.12)$$
$$x^*(T) = x_T > c = \bar{x}_\bullet(T)$$

backward in time, it may be shown that (for certain values of x_T) there exists a positive instant $\hat{t}$ at which the state trajectory $x^*(\cdot)$ reaches the critical price level $\bar{x}_\bullet(\cdot)$. In evaluating the Riccati equation (5.11a) (see, e.g., Davis,[81] pp. 63–66), we restrict our attention to the solution

$$P_\bullet(t) = \frac{z_1 z_2\left(1 - \exp\left[\frac{4b^2k^2(N+1)}{N^2}(z_1 - z_2)(T-t)\right]\right)}{z_2 - z_1 \exp\left[\frac{4b^2k^2(N+1)}{N^2}(z_1 - z_2)(T-t)\right]},$$
$$t \in (\hat{t}, T] \qquad (5.13a)$$

where $z_1 < z_2$ denotes the real, positive roots of the quadratic equation

$$\frac{4b^2k^2(N+1)}{N^2} z^2 - \left(2k + r + \frac{2bk(N+2)}{N}\right) z + 1 = 0 \qquad (5.13b)$$

The game's outcome corresponding to a symmetric play of (5.8) is seen to consist of two phases: In the first phase ($t < \hat{t}$) the oligopolists refrain from production, while in the second ($t > \hat{t}$) production is profitable. The N-tuple of symmetric strategies (5.8) qualifies as a subgame perfect equilibrium. The proof follows by standard application of Theorem 3.1.

A similar pattern can be observed, if the players commit themselves to the use of open-loop decision rules over $[0, T]$. The resulting equilibrium outcome is necessarily symmetric, and its behavior in the interior of $x \geqslant 0$, $u_\bullet \geqslant 0$ can be described by the solution to the following autonomous system:

$$\dot{x} = k[a - 2bu_\bullet - x] \tag{5.14a}$$

$$\dot{u}_\bullet = -(r + 2k)\, x + (c + u_\bullet)(r + k) - 2bku_\bullet (N - 1)/N + ka \tag{5.14b}$$

with boundary conditions

$$x(0) = x_0; \qquad u_\bullet(T) = x(T) - c \tag{5.15}$$

To obtain equation (5.14b) neglect the second term on the right-hand side of expression (4.95).

The phase diagram for this system is depicted in Figure 3. First we observe that the stationary point

$$\begin{aligned} {}^{(k)}x^{\mathrm{s}} &= \frac{2bak + N(a + 2bc)(k + r)}{2bk + N(2b + 1)(k + r)}; \\ {}^{(k)}u_\bullet^{\mathrm{s}} &= \frac{N(a - c)(k + r)}{2bk + N(2b + 1)(k + r)} \end{aligned} \tag{5.16}$$

(which is obviously unique in $x \geqslant 0$, $u_\bullet \geqslant 0$) is a saddlepoint. Two particular trajectories indicated by dotted curves—the *stable branches*—converge toward point (5.16) as $t \to \infty$. Two possible constellations for the initial price level x_0 are illustrated in Figure 3. In each

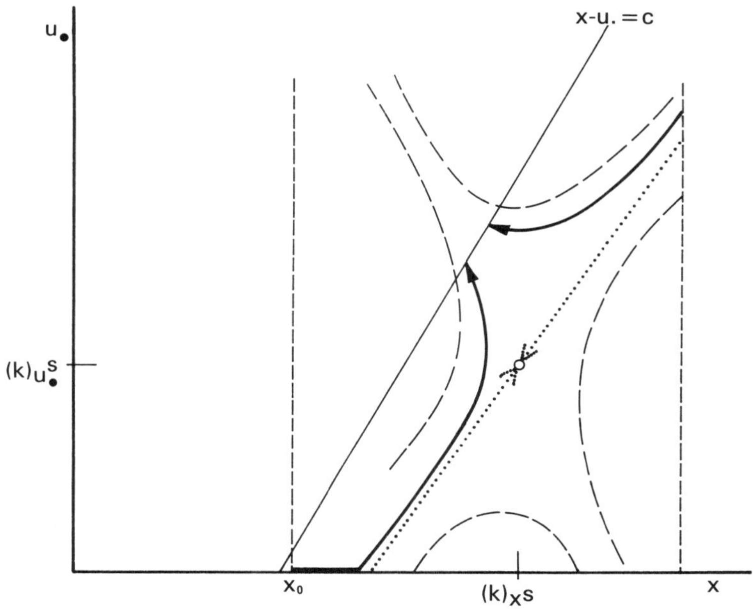

FIGURE 3. The open-loop (equilibrium) outcome to the finite horizon oligopoly game.

case a solution trajectory of system (5.14a,b) starts at $t = 0$ on the line $x = x_0$ and terminates on the line $x - u_{\bullet} = c$ at time T.

If the initial price level is sufficiently small, the corresponding solution calls for an initial phase of inactivity until a critical price level is reached, beyond which the oligopoly is productive. In the infinite horizon game (to be considered in Section 5.1.2) the critical price is indicated by the intersection (point) of the x-axis and the lower stable branch.

The solutions depicted in Figure 3 exhibit the

so-called *turnpike property*. If T is sufficiently large, they move away from their initial values toward the stable manifold (which consists of the two stable branches), staying in its neighborhood except for some final time interval needed to satisfy the terminal conditions. Turnpike results may be derived for the subgame perfect equilibrium as well.[79] The part played by the stable manifold is now undertaken by the subgame perfect equilibrium of the infinite horizon game.

5.2.2. The Infinite Horizon Oligopoly

From Figure 3, we conclude that for the case of an infinite time horizon the open-loop equilibrium outcome exhibits the property of *global asymptotic stability*. The solution is determined by following the stable branch that begins at $x = x_0$ and approaching the saddlepoint asymptotically. If x_0 is sufficiently small, we first follow the x-axis until the critical price level (and the lower stable branch) is reached, and then proceed as above.

Following Fershtman and Kamien,[78] we let $k \to \infty$, i.e., the market price converges instantaneously to the linear demand price $\tilde{x}(t)$. The limit of $({}^{(k)}x^{\mathrm{s}}, {}^{(k)}u^{\mathrm{s}}_{\bullet})$ is then given by

$$ {}^{(\infty)}x^{\mathrm{s}} = \frac{2ba + N(a + 2bc)}{2b + N(2b + 1)}; \qquad {}^{(\infty)}u^{\mathrm{s}}_{\bullet} = \frac{N(a - c)}{2b + N(2b + 1)} \tag{5.17} $$

But ${}^{(\infty)}x^{\mathrm{s}}$ is precisely the price at the equilibrium point $({}^{(\infty)}u^{\mathrm{s}}_{\bullet}, \ldots, {}^{(\infty)}u^{\mathrm{s}}_{\bullet})$ of

$$ \max_{u_i \geq 0} \tilde{x}u_i - cu_i - u_i^2/2, \qquad i = 1, \ldots, N \tag{5.18a} $$

subject to

$$\tilde{x} = a - 2b[u_1 + u_2 + \cdots + u_N]/N; \qquad a > c > 0, \qquad b > 0 \tag{5.18b}$$

a static Cournot (oligopoly) game.

To obtain a symmetric, subgame perfect equilibrium of the infinite horizon oligopoly game, replace in relation (5.8) the time-variant parameters $P_{\bullet}(t)$ [as given by relation (5.13a)] and $v_{\bullet}(t)$ by their limits (as $t \to \infty$)

$$z_1 = \frac{\begin{pmatrix}(2k+r)\,N^2 + 2bkN(N+2) \\ -\sqrt{[(2k+r)\,N^2 + 2bkN(N+2)]^2 - 16b^2k^2N^2(N+1)}\end{pmatrix}}{8b^2k^2(N+1)} \tag{5.19}$$

and

$$w_1 = \frac{k(a+2bc)\,z_1 - c}{r - [4b^2k^2(N+1)/(N)]\,z_1 + (4b+N)\,k/N} \tag{5.20}$$

In the interior of $x \geqslant 0$, $u_{\bullet} \geqslant 0$, the resulting outcome can be described by the solution to the following autonomous system:

$$\dot{x} = k[a - 2bu_{\bullet} - x] \tag{5.21a}$$

$$\dot{u}_{\bullet} = -(r+2k)\,x + (c+u_{\bullet})(r+k) - 2bku_{\bullet}(N-1)/N + ka - k[2b(N-1)/N](x - c - u_{\bullet})(1 - 2bkz_1/N) \tag{5.21b}$$

To obtain equation (5.21b) replace the second term on the right-hand side of expression (4.95) by

$$\frac{\tilde{H}^0_{u_{\bar{\bullet}}} f_{u_\bullet}}{(\tilde{H}^0_{u_\bullet u_\bullet} + \tilde{H}^0_{u_\bullet u_{\bar{\bullet}}})} \frac{\partial \psi^*_\bullet(x)}{\partial x}$$

where

$$\psi^*_\bullet(x) = (1 - 2bkz_1/N)\, x - c - 2bkw_1/N \tag{5.22}$$

The autonomous system (5.21a,b) admits a stationary point

$${}^{(k)}x^{\bar{s}} = \frac{2bak + (a + 2bc)[N(k+r) + (N-1)\, 2bk(1 - 2bkz_1/N)]}{2bk + (2b+1)[N(k+r) + (N-1)\, 2bk(1 - 2bkz_1/N)]} \tag{5.23a}$$

$${}^{(k)}u^{\bar{s}}_\bullet = \frac{(a-c)[N(k+r) + (N-1)\, 2bk(1 - 2bkz_1/N)]}{2bk + (2b+1)[N(k+r) + (N-1)\, 2bk(1 - 2bkz_1/N)]} \tag{5.23b}$$

which is a saddlepoint.

By means of a phase diagram analysis, it is possible to show that the equilibrium output will be greater than in the infinite horizon open-loop case. Due to the process of conditioning their output rate on the observed price, the oligopolists employing (symmetric) subgame perfect equilibrium strategies will deviate from the zero production level at an earlier time instant. For $k \to \infty$ the stationary price ${}^{(k)}x^{\bar{s}}$ converges to a price below ${}^{(\infty)}x^{s}$—the static Cournot equilibrium price.

Remark 5.1. In quite natural to expect that the sufficiency proof for the finite horizon subgame perfect and open-loop equilibria can be carried over to the infinite horizon case. Since

1. any admissible state trajectory is necessarily bounded,
2. the resulting outcomes converge toward a stationary point,

it may be easily shown that the sufficient transversality condition

$$\lim_{T \to \infty} \eta_i(T)[y_i - y_i^*(T)] \geqslant 0 \qquad (3.47d)$$

which implies conditions (3.47b,c), is satisfied.

5.3. R & D Games

Invention is the mother of necessity
Thorstein Veblen

The decision-theoretic approach to dynamic research and development situations has been formulated by Kamien and Schwartz.[82–85] Scherer[86] analyzed R & D resource allocation under rivalry. By using a differential game framework, Reinganum[87,88] synthesized these two basic approaches.

5.3.1. *The Race for Priority*

Consider the following stylized view of the research process.[18,89] N identical firms are engaged in a race for a particular technological breakthrough. Assume that the ith player's completion time is a random variable τ_i with the probability distribution $F_i(t) = \text{Prob}\{\tau_i \leqslant t\}$. It is supposed that the completion times τ_i are mutually independent random variables.

Denote the date of breakthrough by $\tau = \min_i \tau_i$. The player k with $\tau_k = \tau$ is called innovator. By the independency assumption we have

$$F(t) = \text{Prob}\{\tau \leqslant t\} = 1 - \prod_{j=1}^{N} [1 - F_i(t)] \qquad (5.24)$$

Let $u_i(t)$ denote the nonnegative intensity of research effort devoted to the project by firm i. Assume that the hazard rate corresponding to $F_i(t)$, i.e., the conditional probability of success for firm i at time t, is given by

$$\dot{F}_i(t) = \gamma u_i(t)[1 - F_i(t)], \qquad F_i(0) = 0 \qquad (5.25)$$

where γ is a positive constant. Denote by r the common discount rate and by P_{L} the present (constant) value of the innovation to the innovator who wins at time t; P_{F} is the present imitation value. The ith player's expected payoff

$$J_i = \int_0^T \Bigg[P_{\mathrm{L}} \dot{F}_i \prod_{j \neq i} (1 - F_j) + P_{\mathrm{F}} \sum_{j \neq i} \dot{F}_j \prod_{k \neq j} (1 - F_k) - \frac{1}{2} e^{-rt} u_i^2 \prod_{j=1}^{N} (1 - F_j) \Bigg] dt \qquad (5.26a)$$

$$= \int_0^T \left(\gamma P_{\mathrm{L}} u_i + \gamma P_{\mathrm{F}} \sum_{j \neq i} u_j - \frac{1}{2} e^{-rt} u_i^2 \right) \times \prod_{j=1}^{N} (1 - F_j)\, dt \qquad (5.26b)$$

(over a finite time horizon) states that the innovator (or leader) earns the amount P_L at time τ, while the imitator (or follower) earns P_F. Research is costly (and by assumption quadratic). All events are weighted by corresponding probabilities.

To simplify the presentation we introduce the following state transformation:

$$\ln(1 - F_i) = -\gamma x_i$$

The corresponding transformed game is given by

$$\max_{u_i} \int_0^T \exp\left\{-\gamma \sum_{j=1}^{N} x_j(t)\right\} \times \left[\gamma P_L u_i + \gamma P_F \sum_{j \neq i} u_j - \frac{1}{2} e^{-rt} u_i^2\right] dt \quad (5.27a)$$

subject to

$$\dot{x}_i = u_i, \qquad x_i(0) = 0 \quad (5.27b)$$

Remark 5.2. In Reinganum's formulation[87,88] the probability of successfully winning the race for priority by any given date is a function of the accumulated relevant knowledge by that time. The probability of successful completion on or before time t is assumed to be exponential,

$$G_i(z_i) = 1 - \exp\{-\gamma z_i\} \quad (5.28)$$

where $z_i(t)$ denotes total accumulated knowledge by time t, i.e.,

$$z_i(t), \qquad \dot{z}_i(t) = v_i(t)$$

with $v_i(t)$ being the rate at which the ith player acquires knowledge. The resulting differential game is equivalent to game (5.27a,b).

As demonstrated by Reinganum, the exponential differential game (5.27a,b) admits a unique differentiable, subgame perfect (and open-loop type) equilibrium. This means that each player may choose his equilibrium level of research effort independent of accumulated knowledge. However, there exist also other equilibria depending on the state variable.

Apply the following state transformation[18]:

$$y=\exp\left(-\alpha\gamma\sum_{j=1}^{N}x_j\right) \tag{5.29}$$

where α is a nonvanishing constant. The ith player's (transformed) Hamiltonian is now given by

$$H_i=y^{1/\alpha}\left[P_{\mathrm{L}}\gamma u_i+P_{\mathrm{F}}\gamma\sum_{j\neq i}u_j-\frac{1}{2}e^{-rt}u_i^2\right] - \mu_i\alpha\gamma y\sum_{j=1}^{N}u_j$$

Starting from the unique equilibrium of the Hamiltonian game, we may derive the following candidates for a feedback rule equilibrium:

$$u_i^*(t,y,\alpha)=[P_{\mathrm{L}}-\alpha\lambda_i y^{(\alpha-1)/\alpha}]\,\gamma e^{rt}, \qquad i=1,\dots,N \tag{5.30a}$$

where the costate functions $\lambda_i(\cdot)$ satisfy

$$\dot{\lambda}_i=-\frac{\partial H_i}{\partial y}-\sum_{j\neq i}\frac{\partial H_i}{\partial u_j}\frac{\partial u_j^*}{\partial y}, \qquad \lambda_i(T)=0 \tag{5.30b}$$

To any candidate given by system (5.30a,b) there corresponds an open-loop representation evaluated at $y = y^*$, where

$$y^* = \exp\left\{-\alpha\gamma \sum_{j=1}^{N} x_j^*\right\}, \qquad \dot{x}_i^* = u_i^*(t, y^*, \alpha), \qquad x_i^*(0) = 0 \tag{5.31}$$

From relations (5.30a,b) and (5.31) we derive the following uncountable set of (distinct) open-loop representations:

$$u_i^*(t, y^*, \alpha) = -b(t, \alpha)\,\gamma e^{rt} \tag{5.32}$$

with $b(\cdot, \alpha)$ satisfying the scalar Riccati equation

$$\begin{aligned}\dot{b} = \gamma^2 e^{rt}\{&-b^2[\alpha(N-1)+\tfrac{1}{2}]\\ &+b(N-1)[\alpha P_{\mathrm{F}}-(2\alpha-1)\,P_{\mathrm{L}}] \\ &+(N-1)(\alpha-1)\,P_{\mathrm{L}}(P_{\mathrm{F}}-P_{\mathrm{L}})\}\end{aligned} \tag{5.33a}$$

$$b(T, \alpha) = -P_{\mathrm{L}} \tag{5.33b}$$

Note that the outcomes corresponding to the feedback rules (5.31a,b) may be described by ordinary differential equations containing control terms only. This is solely due to the perfectness and qualitative solvability of game (5.27a,b). For $\alpha = 1$ the unique, differentiable subgame perfect equilibrium is obtained. This solution is characterized in the following section.

5.3.2. *Market Structure and Research Intensity*

Solving the differential equation (5.33a,b) for $\alpha = 1$, we obtain the following result:

$$b(t, 1) = -\frac{2(N-1)(P_L - P_F)\, P_L}{\left(\begin{array}{l} (2N-1)\, P_L - [P_L + 2(N-1)\, P_F] \\ \qquad \times \exp\{(P_L - P_F)(N-1)\, \gamma^2 (e^{rt} - e^{rT})/r\} \end{array} \right)} \tag{5.34a}$$

When rewards are completely nonappropriable ($P_F = P_L = P$), $b(\cdot, 1)$ is given by

$$b(t, 1) = \frac{2P}{2 - (2N-1)\, P\gamma^2 (e^{rt} - e^{rT})/r} \tag{5.34b}$$

Comparative static results, which may be stated by simply differentiating relation (5.32) with respect to the parameter in question, can be summarized[(87)] as follows:

1. For $P_L > P_F$, increasing innovation (imitation) rewards stimulate player i to proceed at a higher (smaller) rate of research.
2. The availability of perfect patent protection ($P_F = 0$) will accelerate the development of the innovation.
3. For $P_F = 0$, an increase in the number of players tends to hasten technological breakthrough.

We leave it as an exercise for the reader to prove these claims.

5.4. Fishery Games

> The old alone may comprehend
> a sense in my decree,
> but—if you find a fish on land,
> oh throw it in the sea.
> G. K. Chesterton

The arithmetics of commons[90] applies in a frightening way to the intensive exploitation of fishery resources. Above some level of use—which may be interpreted as change from monopolistic or cartel behavior to a oligopoly or even free access market of individual producers—each "player"s' equilibrium harvest level contributes to each player's economic losses.

In the following section, we deal with a fishery game allowing us to consider the polar cases of monopoly and oligopolistic competition. Our main objective is in analyzing the effects of changes in market structure on the level of conservation and the price profiles for the fishery resource.

5.4.1. The Oligopolistic Fishery Game

Consider the following oligopolistic fishery game:

$$\max_{u_i \geqslant 0} \int_0^\infty e^{-rt} \left[p\left(\sum_{j=1}^N u_j \right) - c(x) \right] u_i \, dt, \qquad i = 1, \dots, N \tag{5.35a}$$

subject to

$$\dot{x} = G(x) - \sum_{j=1}^N u_j; \qquad x(0) = x_0 > 0 \tag{5.35b}$$

$$x \geqslant 0 \tag{5.35c}$$

Here r is a (positive) discount rate, $x(t)$ is the fish population at time t, and u_i denotes the ith player's harvest rate. The (inverse) demand curve $p(\cdot)$, with

$$\frac{\partial p}{\partial u_i} < 0, \qquad u_i \frac{\partial^2 p}{\partial u_i^2} < -2 \frac{\partial p}{\partial u_i} \tag{5.36}$$

defines the price at which consumers will purchase the total catch (per unit time). The function $c(\cdot)$, with

$$c'(x) \leqslant 0, \qquad c''(x) \geqslant 0 \tag{5.37}$$

denotes the cost of a unit harvest when the population level is x. $G(x)$, a natural growth function, is assumed to satisfy conditions (1.23) and

$$G'(0) \in (r, \infty), \qquad G''(x) < 0 \tag{5.38}$$

Define the current value Hamiltonians

$$\begin{aligned} \tilde{H}_i := e^{rt} H_i = \left[p\left(\sum_{j=1}^{N} u_j \right) - c(x) \right] u_i \\ + v_i \left[G(x) - \sum_{j=1}^{N} u_j \right] = \tilde{L}_i + v_i f \end{aligned}$$

The maximum of $\tilde{H}_i$ with respect to $u_i \geqslant 0$ satisfies the following relation:

$$\left. \begin{aligned} u_i &= 0 \\ -\tilde{L}_{u_i}/f_{u_i} = \mathrm{MR}_i - c(x) &= v_i \end{aligned} \right\} \quad \text{if} \quad v_i \begin{Bmatrix} \geqslant \\ < \end{Bmatrix} p\left(\sum_{j \neq i} u_j \right) - c(x) \tag{5.39}$$

where MR_i denotes the ith player's marginal revenue, i.e.,

$$\mathrm{MR}_i = \frac{\partial[p(\sum_{j=1}^{N} u_j)\, u_i]}{\partial u_i} = p\left(\sum_{j=1}^{N} u_j\right) + p'\left(\sum_{j=1}^{N} u_j\right) u_i \tag{5.40}$$

From condition (5.36) it is easily seen that $v_i < p(\sum_{j \neq i} u_j) - c(x)$ will hold if (and only if) the ith player's maximizing control is strictly positive.

By expressing equation (5.40) in terms of a symmetric outcome we obtain

$$\mathrm{MR}_\bullet(u_\bullet) = p(Nu_\bullet) + p'(Nu_\bullet)\, u_\bullet \tag{5.41}$$

$$\mathrm{MR}'_\bullet(u_\bullet) = (N+1)\, p'(Nu_\bullet) + Np''(Nu_\bullet)\, u_\bullet \tag{5.42}$$

In the interior of the region $u_\bullet \geqslant 0$; $x \geqslant 0$, the autonomous system of differential equations is now given by

$$\dot{x} = G(x) - Nu_\bullet \tag{5.43a}$$

$$\dot{u}_\bullet = \frac{\begin{pmatrix} c'(x)[G(x) - (N-1)\, u_\bullet] \\ \quad + [r - G'(x)][\mathrm{MR}_\bullet(u_\bullet) - c(x)] \end{pmatrix}}{\mathrm{MR}'_\bullet(u_\bullet)} + \frac{(N-1)\, c'(x)[p(Nu_\bullet) - c(x)]}{[\mathrm{MR}'_\bullet(u_\bullet)]^2} \tag{5.43b}$$

Setting $\dot{x} = 0$ and $\dot{u}_\bullet = 0$, we obtain the following isoclines:

$$u_\bullet = G(x)/N \tag{5.44a}$$

$$r = G'(x) - \frac{\begin{pmatrix} c'(x)\{G(x) - (N-1)\,u_\bullet \\ \quad + (N-1)[p(Nu_\bullet) - c(x)]\,\mathrm{MR}'_\bullet(u_\bullet)\} \end{pmatrix}}{\mathrm{MR}_\bullet(u_\bullet) - c(x)} \tag{5.44b}$$

In Figure 4, we have undergone the Sisyphean task of gaining some insight into the qualitative behavior of the

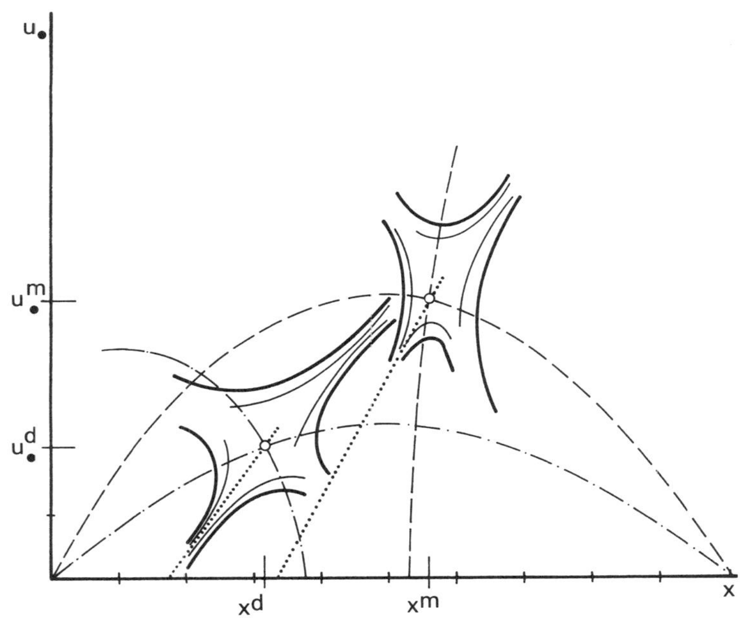

FIGURE 4. Symmetric (equilibrium) outcomes to the fishery game under monopolistic and duopolistic market structures.

solutions of equations (5.43a,b). To make matters as simple as possible choose

$$G(x) = x\left(1 - \frac{x}{10}\right); \qquad p(Nu) = 20 - Nu; \qquad c(x) = 10 - x$$

First we observe that the stationary points $(x^{\mathrm{d}}, u_{\bullet}^{\mathrm{d}})$ —for the duopoly case; $N = 2$—and $(x^{\mathrm{m}}, u_{\bullet}^{\mathrm{m}})$—for the monopoly case; $N = 1$—are saddlepoints. We conclude therefore that the symmetric equilibrium outcome $(N = 2)$ is determined by following the (dotted) stable branch that begins at $x = x_0$ and approaching $(x^{\mathrm{d}}, u_{\bullet}^{\mathrm{d}})$ asymptotically. If x_0 is sufficiently small, we first follow the x-axis until the lower stable branch is reached, and then proceed as above. The optimal solution in the monopoly case shows a similar behavior with respect to $(x^{\mathrm{m}}, u_{\bullet}^{\mathrm{m}})$.

The duopolistic equilibrium harvest is easily compared with the monopolistic extraction policy. In the long run, a duopoly generates a greater price level than a monopolist would do. Nevertheless, the level of conservation in the former case is greater than in the latter. We conclude that, as expected, the oligopolistic fishery results in overfishing.

5.4.2. Extinction, Conservation, and Economic Regulation

Clemhout and Wan[(70)] use a similar game formulation which is consistent with the extinction of the fish population. Their problem is the following:

$$\max_{u_i} \int_{t_0}^{\infty} e^{-rt} L(u_i)\, dt, \qquad i = 1, \ldots, N \qquad (5.45\text{a})$$

subject to

$$\dot{x} = G(x) - \sum_{j=1}^{N} u_j; \qquad x(t_0) = x_0 \tag{5.45b}$$

$L(\cdot)$ represents the ith player's utility of use, or, equivalently, a sale revenue

$$L(u_i) = u_i\, p(u_i) \tag{5.46}$$

where $p(\cdot)$ denotes an inverse demand function.

The authors' main concern is to illustrate that—in certain situations to be described below—extinction may occur in finite time under an oligopolistic market structure, while survival is ensured as the effect of cartelization.

Introduce the following critical assumptions:

1. $L(0) = 0; \qquad L'(0) \in (0, \infty), \qquad L'' < 0$ (5.47a)
2. $Nr < G'(0) < \infty$ (5.47b)

Translating equations (4.88) and (4.89) into a current value formulation, a time-invariant, symmetric feedback equilibrium can be described by the following relation:

$$\frac{du_{\bullet}^{*}}{dx} = \frac{G'(x) - r}{\begin{pmatrix} (N-1) + [G(x) - Nu_{\bullet}^{*}(x)] \\ \times [-L''(u_{\bullet}^{*}(x))/L'(u_{\bullet}^{*}(x))] \end{pmatrix}} \tag{5.48}$$

Since we have to consider the possibility of extinction after some finite time, the infinite horizon game (5.45a,b) should be partitioned into a free time problem with terminal condition

$$t_f := \min\{t \geqslant 0 \mid x(t) = 0\} \tag{5.49}$$

and a remaining trivial game over (t_f, ∞), where $x \equiv u_\bullet^*(x) \equiv 0$, identically.

Suppose that an optimal terminal point, say, T^* exists. Then the following necessary condition follows from relations (3.19h) and (3.22):

$$L(u_\bullet^*[x(T^*)]) = 0 \tag{5.50}$$

From conditions (5.47a), (5.49), and (5.50), we conclude that

$$u_\bullet^*(0) = 0 \tag{5.51}$$

It can be established[70] from this boundary condition, relations (5.48) and (5.47b) that there exists an $\tilde{x} > 0$ such that (in equilibrium) any initial population level $x_0 \in (0, \tilde{x})$ is condemned to decline.

Since $L'(0) < \infty$, extinction occurs after a finite period of time. The initial condition $(x_0, u_\bullet^*(x_0))$ to the autonomous system

$$\dot{x}_\bullet = G(x_\bullet) - Nu_\bullet \tag{5.52a}$$

$$\dot{u}_\bullet = \frac{[G(x_\bullet) - Nu_\bullet][G'(x_\bullet) - r]}{\begin{pmatrix}(N-1) + [G(x_\bullet) - Nu_\bullet^*(x_\bullet)] \\ \times [-L''(u_\bullet^*(x_\bullet))/L'(u_\bullet^*(x_\bullet))]\end{pmatrix}} \tag{5.52b}$$

is obtained by integrating function (5.48) with boundary

condition (5.51) over $[0, x_0]$. The solution to system (5.52a,b) approaches the stationary point (0, 0) monotonically.

For $N=1$, the differential game (5.45a,b) degenerates to an optimal control problem describing the case of a cartel or sole ownership. Clemhout and Wan[70] illustrate that, under assumptions (1) and (2), extinction never happens.

Various alternative methods of fishery conservation and regulation have been discussed in the literature. These include total catch quotas,[23] taxes on catch and licenses,[91] etc. The effect of such methods can also be analyzed by using a (differential) game-theoretic framework. To achieve, say, allocated player quotas Q_i, $i=1,\ldots, N$, it would be necessary to adjoin N additional state variables y_i under the dynamic constraints

$$\dot{y}_i = u_i; \qquad y_i(0)=0; \qquad y_i(T)=Q_i \tag{5.53}$$

to a finite horizon variant of game (5.35a,b,c).

Exercises

5.1. Compare the subgame-perfect solutions to Faust's game under hierarchical and simultaneous play.

5.2. A habitual shoplifter's[92,93] objective is to maximize

$$J_1 = \int_0^T [C_1(u_1)(1-x) - k_1 x]\, dt$$

where $C_1(\cdot)$ is the instantaneous utility derived from his pilfering rate u_1 and k_1 denotes a lump sum penalty at the instant he is caught. The state variable x—the probability of the thief's getting caught by time t—is given by

$$\dot{x} = u_1 u_2(1-x), \qquad x(0) = x_0$$

where u_2 denotes the law enforcement rate. The police headquarter's objective is to minimize

$$J_2 = \int_0^T [C_2(u_2)(1-x) - k_2 x]\, dt$$

where $C_2(\cdot)$ denotes the cost of law enforcement and k_2 is a premium at the instant the thief is being caught.
Solve this (qualitatively solvable) game under the assumptions

$$C_1(u_1) = c_1 u_1^{\alpha}, \qquad \text{with} \quad c_1 > 0, \qquad 0 < \alpha < 1$$
$$C_2(u_2) = c_2 u_2^{\beta}, \qquad \text{with} \quad \beta > 1$$

(*Hint:* See Feichtinger.[93] Other unusual problems are given in Feichtinger and Mehlmann.[94])

5.3. Prove the comparative static results stated at the end of Section 5.3.

5.4. Recall the R & D game of Section 5.3.1, and suppose that knowledge is transmittable and transferable.[88] Replace the dynamic constraint (5.27b) by

$$\dot{x}_i = u_i + \kappa \sum_{j \neq i} u_j, \qquad x_i(0) = 0$$

where κ is the fraction of knowledge shared with the others. Characterize the corresponding unique, differentiable and subgame perfect equilibrium and compare its counterpart (5.32) and (5.34a,b).

5.5. Consider the following differential game model[95] of competitive dynamic advertising:

$$\max_{u_1 \geqslant 0} \int_0^T e^{-r_1 t}[q_1 x - (c_1/2)\, u_1^2]\, dt + e^{-r_1 T} S_1 x(T)$$

$$\max_{u_2 \geqslant 0} \int_0^T e^{-r_2 t}[q_2(1-x) - (c_2/2)\, u_2^2]\, dt + e^{-r_2 T} S_2(1 - x(T))$$

subject to

$$\dot{x} = u_1 \sqrt{1-x} - u_2 \sqrt{x}; \qquad x(0) = x_0$$

where x denotes the market share of firm 1 at time t, $1-x$ the market share of firm 2 at time t. The ith player's advertising rate is given by u_i, the unit margin and the cost parameter by $q_i > 0$ and $c_i > 0$, respectively. The firms ascribe values to their market shares at terminal time T. Show that a subgame perfect equilibrium (under simultaneous play) is given by

$$\psi_1^*(t, x) = \eta_1(t) \sqrt{1-x}/c_1; \qquad \psi_2^*(t, x) = \eta_2 \sqrt{x}/c_2$$

with $\eta_i(\cdot)$, $i = 1, 2$ $(j \neq i)$ satisfying

$$\dot{\eta}_i = r_i \eta_i - q_i + \eta_i^2/(2c_i) + \eta_i \eta_j / c_j; \qquad \eta_i(T) = S_i$$

5.6. Discuss the structural properties of the game defined in Exercise 5.5. Characterize the subgame perfect equilibrium by making use of a phase diagram analysis of the two-dimensional system $(\dot{\eta}_1, \dot{\eta}_2)$.

5.7. Recall the "Eskimoean" fishery game of Example 3.4 and Exercise 4.7. Characterize the (equilibrium) outcomes corresponding to the extensive situations (2.50) and (3.48) by means of phase diagram analysis.

References

1. J. von Neumann and O. Morgenstern, *Theory of Games and Economic Behavior*, Princeton University Press, Princeton (1947).
2. R. Isaacs, *Differential Games*, Kreiger Publishing Company, Huntington, New York (1975).
3. L. D. Berkovitz, in: *Advances in Game Theory* (M. Dresher, L. S. Shapley, and A. W. Tucker, eds.), pp. 127–174, Princeton University Press, Princeton (1964).
4. G. Leitmann and G. Mon, Some geometric aspects of differential games, *J. Astronaut. Sci.* **14**, 56 (1967).
5. L. S. Pontryagin, On the theory of differential games, *Uspekhi Mat. Nauk* **21**, 219–274 (1966).
6. A. Zaubermann, *Differential Games and Other Game-Theoretic Topics in Soviet Literature*, New York University Press, New York (1975).
7. P. Varaiya and Y. Lin, Existence of saddlepoint in differential games, *SIAM J. Control* **7**, 141–157 (1969).
8. A. Friedman, *Differential Games*, Wiley, New York (1971).
9. N. N. Krasovsky and A. I. Subbotin, *Jeux Différentiels*, Mir, Moscow (1977).
10. J. Case, Towards a theory of many player differential games, *SIAM J. Control* **7**(2), 179–197 (1969).
11. J. Case, in: *Differential Games and Related Topics* (H. W. Kuhn

and G. P. Szegö, eds.), pp. 345–371, North-Holland, Amsterdam (1971).
12. M. Shubik, *Game Theory in the Social Sciences—Concepts and Solutions*, The MIT Press, Cambridge (1982).
13. J. W. Friedman, *Game Theory with Applications to Economics*, Oxford University Press, New York (1986).
14. J. Case, *Economics and the Competitive Process*, New York University Press, New York (1979).
15. E. M. Vaisbord and Z. Zhukovsky, *Introduction to Many Player Differential Games and Their Applications* (in Russian), Sovetskoe Radio, Moscow (1980).
16. T. Başar and G. J. Olsder, *Dynamic Noncooperative Game Theory*, Academic Press, London (1982).
17. L. A. Petrosyan and G. V. Tomsky, *Dynamic Games and Their Applications* (in Russian), Izdatelstvo Leningradskogo Universiteta, Leningrad (1982).
18. A. Mehlmann, *Differentialspiele—Die Analyse dynamischer Konfliktsituationen*, Hain Scientific, Königstein (1985).
19. A. Mehlmann and R. Willing, Eine spieltheoretische Interpretation des Faustmotivs, *Optimization* **15**(2), 243–252 (1984).
20. K. Lancaster, The dynamic inefficiency of capitalism, *J. Pol. Econ.* **81**, 1092–1109 (1973).
21. G. Leitmann and P. T. Liu, A differential game model of labor–management negotiation during strike, *J. Optim. Theory Appl.* **13**(4), 427–435 (1974).
22. M. Simaan and T. Takayama, Game theory applied to dynamic duopoly problems with production constraints, *Automatica* **14**, 161–166 (1978).
23. C. W. Clark, in: *Dynamic Optimization and Mathematical Economics* (P. Liu, ed.), pp. 117–132, Plenum Press, New York (1980).
24. H. W. Kuhn, in: *Contributions to the Theory of Games ii* (H. W. Kuhn and A. W. Tucker, eds.), pp. 193–216, Princeton University Press, Princeton (1953).
25. A. Mäkelä, Differential games in evolutionary theory: Height growth strategies of trees, *Theor. Popul. Biol.* **27**, 239–267 (1985).
26. H. S. Witsenhausen, On information structures, feedback and causality, *SIAM J. Control* **9**, 149–160 (1971).
27. H. S. Witsenhausen, in: *The Theory and Application of Differential Games* (J. D. Grote, ed.), pp. 77–84, D. Reidel, Dordrecht (1975).

28. J. C. Harsanyi, Rationality postulates for bargaining solutions in cooperative and non-cooperative games, *Manage. Sci.* **9**, 141–153 (1962).
29. N. Howard, *Paradoxes of Rationality: Theory of Metagames and Political Behavior*, The MIT Press, Cambridge (1971).
30. M. I. Kamien and N. L. Schwartz, *Dynamic Optimization—The Calculus of Variations and Optimal Control in Economics and Management*, North-Holland, Amsterdam (1981).
31. S. P. Sethi and G. L. Thompson, *Optimal Control Theory Applications to Management Science*, Martinus Nijhoff, Boston (1981).
32. G. Feichtinger and R. F. Hartl, *Optimale Kontrolle ökonomischer Prozesse*, de Gruyter, Berlin (1986).
33. A. Seierstad and K. Sydsæter, *Optimal Control Theory with Economic Applications*, North-Holland, Amsterdam (1987).
34. J. C. Harsanyi, *Rational Behavior and Bargaining Equilibrium in Games and Social Situations*, Cambridge University Press, Cambridge (1977).
35. R. Selten, Reexamination of the perfectness concept for equilibrium points in extensive games, *Int. J. Game Theory* **4**, 25–55 (1975).
36. W. H. Fleming and R. W. Rishel, *Deterministic and Stochastic Optimal Control*, Springer-Verlag, Berlin (1975).
37. R. Radner, Collusive behavior in noncooperative epsilon-equilibria of oligopolies with long but finite lives, *J. Econ. Theory* **22**, 136–154 (1980).
38. B. Tołwinski, A. Haurie, and G. Leitmann, Cooperative equilibria in differential games, *Proceedings of the American Control Conference*, San Francisco (1983).
39. C. Fershtman, Structural and behavioral dynamics in multiperiod oligopolistic games, *Research Paper*, Economics Department, The Hebrew University, Jerusalem 91905 (1986).
40. P. T. Liu, Nonzero-sum differential games with bargaining solutions, *J. Optim. Theory Appl.* **11**(3), 284–292 (1973).
41. P. T. Liu, Optimal threat strategies in differential games, *J. Math. Anal. Appl.* **43**, 161–169 (1973).
42. A. Haurie, A note on nonzero-sum differential games with bargaining solutions, *J. Optim. Theory Appl.* **18**(1), 31–39 (1976).
43. H. Stalford and G. Leitmann, in: *Topics in Differential Games* (A. Blaquière, ed.), pp. 345–376, North-Holland, Amsterdam (1973).

44. L. D. Berkovitz, Necessary conditions for optimal strategies in a class of differential games and control problems, *SIAM J. Control* **5**, 1–24 (1967).
45. A. Blaquière, F. Gérard, and G. Leitmann, *Quantitative and Qualitative Games*, Academic Press, New York (1971).
46. G. Leitmann, *Cooperative and Non-Cooperative Many Player Differential Games*, Springer-Verlag, Vienna (1974).
47. I. G. Sarma, R. K. Ragade, and V. R. Prassad, Necessary conditions for optimal strategies in a class of noncooperative N-person differential games, *SIAM J. Control* **7**, 637–644 (1969).
48. C. C. von Weizsäcker, Existence of optimal programs of accumulation for an infinite time horizon, *Rev. Econ. Stud.* **32**, 85–104 (1965).
49. D. Gale, On optimal development in a multi-sector economy, *Rev. Econ. Stud.* **34**, 1–18 (1967).
50. H. Halkin, Necessary conditions for optimal control problems with infinite horizons, *Econometrica* **42**, 267–272 (1974).
51. H. Moulin, *Game Theory for the Social Sciences*, New York University Press, New York (1982).
52. T. Başar and A. Haurie, in: *Advances in Large Scale Systems*, Vol. 1 (J. B. Cruz, ed.), pp. 163–201, JAI Press, Greenwich (1984).
53. J. B. Cruz, Survey of Nash and Stackelberg equilibrium strategies in dynamic games, *Ann. Econ. Soc. Meas.* **4**(2), 339–344 (1975).
54. G. P. Papavassilopoulos and J. B. Cruz, Nonclassical control problems and Stackelberg games, *IEEE Trans. Autom. Control* **24**(2), 155–165 (1979).
55. E. Dockner, G. Feichtinger, and A. Mehlmann, Noncooperative solutions for a differential game model of fishery, *Research Report 65*, Department of Operations Research, University of Technology, Vienna (1984).
56. M. Pohjola, in: *Dynamic Games and Applications in Economics* (T. Başar, ed.), pp. 103–133, Springer-Verlag, Berlin (1986).
57. T. Başar and G. J. Olsder, Team-optimal closed-loop Stackelberg strategies in hierarchical control problems, *Automatica* **16**, 409–414 (1980).
58. M. Pohjola, Nash and Stackelberg solutions in a differential game model of capitalism, *J. Econ. Dyn. Control* **6**, 173–186 (1983).
59. S. Clemhout and H. Y. Wan, A class of trilinear games, *J. Optim. Theory Appl.* **14**(4), 419–424 (1974).

60. G. Leitmann and W. E. Schmitendorf, Profit maximization through advertising: A nonzero sum differential game approach, *IEEE Trans. Autom. Control* **23**, 646–650 (1978).
61. J. F. Reinganum, A class of differential games for which the open-loop and closed-loop equilibria coincide, *J. Optim. Theory Appl.* **36**(2), 453–462 (1982).
62. A. Mehlmann and R. Willing, On nonunique closed-loop Nash equilibria for a class of differential games with a unique and degenerate feedback solution, *J. Optim. Theory Appl.* **41**(3), 463–472 (1983).
63. C. Fershtman, Identification of classes of differential games for which the open-loop is a degenerated feedback Nash equilibrium, *J. Optim. Theory Appl.* **55**(2), 217–231 (1987).
64. T. Başar, Informationally nonunique equilibrium solutions in differential games, *SIAM J. Control Optim.* **15**(4), 636–660 (1977).
65. T. Başar and H. Selbuz, Properties of Nash solutions of a two-stage nonzero-sum game, *IEEE Trans. Autom. Control* **21**, 48–54 (1976).
66. T. Eisele, Nonexistence and nonuniqueness of open-loop equilibria in linear-quadratic differential games, *J. Optim. Theory Appl.* **37**(4), 443–467 (1982).
67. M. Simaan and J. B. Cruz, On the Stackelberg strategy in nonzero-sum games, *J. Optim. Theory Appl.* **11**(5), 533–555 (1973).
68. E. Dockner, G. Feichtinger, and S. Jørgensen, Tractable classes of non-zerosum open-loop differential games, *J. Optim. Theory Appl.* **45**(2), 179–197 (1985).
69. G. Feichtinger, The Nash solution of an advertising differential game: generalization of a model by Leitmann and Schmitendorf, *IEEE Trans. Autom. Control* **28**, 1044–1048 (1983).
70. S. Clemhout and H. Y. Wan, in: *Optimal Control Theory and Economic Analysis 2* (G. Feichtinger, ed.), pp. 549–568, North-Holland, Amsterdam (1984).
71. S. J. Brams, *Biblical Games: A Strategic Analysis of Stories in the Old Testament*, The MIT Press, Cambridge (1980).
72. I. Lalu, in: *The Formal Study of Drama* (*Poetics 6*, S. Marcus, ed.), pp. 339–350, North-Holland, Amsterdam (1977).
73. A. Rapoport, *Fights, Games and Debates*, The University of Michigan Press, Ann Arbor (1960).
74. P. Teodorescu-Brînzeu, in: *The Formal Study of Drama* (*Poetics 6*, S. Marcus, ed.), pp. 351–374, North-Holland, Amsterdam (1977).

75. N. N. Vorobyev, in: *Togetherness of Sciences and the Secrets of Artistic Creation* (in Russian), pp. 348–372, Izkustvo, Moscow (1968).
76. S. J. Brams, *Superior Beings: If They Exist, How Would We Know*, Springer, New York (1983).
77. G. C. Evans, The dynamics of monopoly, *Am. Math. Monthly* **31**, 75–83 (1924).
78. C. Fershtman and M. I. Kamien, Dynamic duopolistic competition with sticky prices, *Econometrica* **55**(5), 1151–1164 (1987).
79. C. Fershtman and M. I. Kamien, Turnpike properties in a dynamic duopoly with sticky prices, Working paper, Department of Managerial Economics and Decision Sciences, J. L. Kellog Graduate School of Management, Northwestern University, Evanston, Illinois 60201 (1985).
80. M. Shubik, *A Game-Theoretic Approach to Political Economy*, MIT Press, Cambridge (1986).
81. H. T. Davis, *Introduction to Nonlinear Differential and Integral Equations*, Dover, New York (1962).
82. M. I. Kamien and N. L. Schwartz, Expenditure patterns for risky R & D projects, *J. Appl. Prob.* **8**, 60–73 (1971).
83. M. I. Kamien and N. L. Schwartz, Timing of innovations under rivaly, *Econometrica* **40**, 43–60 (1972).
84. M. I. Kamien and N. L. Schwartz, Risky R & D with rivalry, *Ann. Econ. Soc. Meas.* **3**, 267–277 (1974).
85. M. I. Kamien and N. L. Schwartz, *Market Structure and Innovation*, Cambridge University Press, Cambridge (1982).
86. F. M. Scherer, Research and development resource allocation under rivalry, *Quart. J. Econ.* **81**, 359–394 (1967).
87. J. F. Reinganum, A dynamic game of R & D: Patent protection and competitive behavior, *Econometrica* **50**, 671–688 (1982).
88. J. F. Reinganum, Dynamic games of innovation, *J. Econ. Theory* **25**, 21–41 (1981).
89. G. Feichtinger, in: *Optimal Control Theory and Economic Analysis* (G. Feichtinger, ed.), pp. 373–398, North-Holland, Amsterdam (1982).
90. G. Hardin, The tragedy of the commons, *Science* **162**, 1243–1248 (1968).
91. C. W. Clark, Towards a predictive model for the economic regulation of commercial fisheries, *Can. J. Fish. Aquat. Sci.* **37**, 1111–1129 (1980).

92. S. P. Sethi, Optimal pilfering policies for dynamic continuous thieves, *Manage. Sci.* **25**(6), 535–542 (1979).
93. G. Feichtinger, A differential games solution to a model of competition between a thief and the police, *Manage. Sci.* **29**(6), 686–699 (1983).
94. G. Feichtinger and A. Mehlmann, Planning the unusual: Applications of control theory to nonstandard problems, *Acta Applicandae Mathematicae* **7**, 79–102 (1986).
95. G. Sorger, Competitive dynamic advertising: A modification of the Case game, *J. Econ. Dyn. Control* (to appear).

Selected Bibliography

The following references are suggested to the reader who wishes to familiarize himself more thoroughly with the areas of application of nonzero-sum differential games.

Advertising and Pricing

E. Dockner, Optimal pricing of a monopoly against a competitive producer, *Optim. Control Appl. Methods* **5**(4), 345–352 (1984).

E. Dockner and G. Feichtinger, in: *Dynamic Games and Applications in Economics* (T. Başar, ed.), pp. 238–251, Springer-Verlag, Berlin (1986).

E. Dockner and S. Jørgensen, Cooperative and non-cooperative differential game solutions to an investment and pricing problem, *J. Oper. Res. Soc.* **35**(8), 731–739 (1984).

G. Feichtinger, in: *Operations Research Proceedings* (B. Fleischman *et al.*, eds.), pp. 636–644, Springer-Verlag, Berlin (1982).

G. Feichtinger and E. Dockner, Optimal pricing in a duopoly: A non-cooperative differential games solution, *J. Optim. Theory Appl.* **45**(2), 199–218 (1985).

M. T. Flaherty, Dynamic limit pricing, barriers to entry, and rational firms, *J. Econ. Theory* **23**, 160–182 (1980).

J. Gaugusch, The non-cooperative solution of a differential game: Advertising versus pricing, *Optim. Control Appl. Methods* **5**, 353–360 (1984).

S. Jørgensen, A survey of some differential games in advertising, *J. Econ. Dyn. Control* **4**, 341–369 (1982).

G. L. Thompson and Jian-Tsair Teng, Optimal pricing and advertising policies for new product oligopoly models, *Marketing Science* **3**(2), 148–168 (1984).

Arms Race and Battle Games

D. L. Brito, A dynamic model of an armaments race, *Int. Econ. Rev.* **13**, 359–375 (1972).

S. Deger and S. Sen, Optimal control and differential game models of military expenditure in less developed countries, *J. Econ. Dyn. Control* **7**, 153–169 (1984).

J. V. Gillespie, D. A. Zinnes, and G. S. Tahim, Foreign military assistance and the armaments race: A differential game model with control, *The Papers of the Peace Science Society* **25**, 35–51 (1975).

M. D. Intrilgator and D. L. Brito, Can arms races lead to the outbreak of war?, *J. Conf. Resolut.* **28**(1), 63–84 (1984).

J. G. Taylor, Differential-game examinations of optimal time-sequential fire-support strategies, *Nav. Res. Logist. Q.* **25**, 323–356 (1978).

Macroeconomics

A. Bagchi, *Stackelberg Differential Games in Economic Models*, Springer-Verlag, Berlin (1984).
S. Clemhout and H. Y. Wan, Interactive economic dynamics and differential games, *J. Optim. Theory Appl.* **27**(1), 7–30 (1979).
H. Myoken, Non-zero-sum differential games for the balance-of-payments adjustments in an open economy, *Int. J. Syst. Sci.* **6**, 501–511 (1975).
R. Neck, in: *Optimal Control Theory and Economic Analysis 2* (G. Feichtinger, ed.), pp. 607–632, North-Holland, Amsterdam (1985).
L. F. Pau, A differential game among sectors in a macroeconomy, *Automatica* **11**, 473–485 (1975).

Resource Economics

T. R. Fischer, A hierarchical game approach to fishery resource management, *IEEE Trans. Syst., Man Cybern.* **11**, 216–222 (1981).
V. Kaitala, in: *Dynamic Games and Applications in Economics* (T. Başar, ed.), pp. 252–266, Springer-Verlag, Berlin (1986).
J. F. Reinganum and N. L. Stokey, Oligopoly extraction of a common property natural resource: The impor-

tance of the period of commitment in dynamic games, *Int. Econ. Rev.* **26**, 161–172 (1985).

S. W. Salant, Exhaustible resources and industrial structure: A Nash–Cournot approach to the world oil market, *J. Pol. Econ.* **84**, 1079–1093 (1976).

J. E. Stiglitz and P. Dasgupta, Market structure and resource extraction under uncertainty, *Scand. J. Econom.*, 318–333 (1981).

Index

Action
  normal form, 43, 44
  simultaneous, 43, 65
  space, 31
Advertising, 132
  effectiveness, 132
  expenditure, 132
Advertising game, 131–134
Attainable set, 77, 78
Auden, W. H., 162

Bargaining schemes, 70
Başar, T., 32, 100, 109, 117, 118, 127
Bellman, R., 31, 73
Bellman equation: *see* Dynamic programming
Berkovitz, L., 17, 86
Best response, 102, 127
  follower's, 99
  set, 97
Bijective transformation, 29
Binding agreement, 42, 49
Blaquiére, A., 86
Brams, S. J., 155, 160

Capitalism, Lancaster's paradigm of, 22; *See* Game, of capitalism
Carroll, L., 73
"Carrying capacity", 26
Catchability coefficient, 26
Closure, 29, 82
Chesterton, G. K., 179
Clark, C. W., 25, 106
Clemhout, S., 113, 129, 148, 183, 186
Commitment, 43
  enforceable, 42
Communication, 64
  preplay, 42, 49
Compact, with the devil, 18
Competition
  between firms, 132
  model of duopolistic, 24
Conan-Doyle, A., 155

Condition
  initial state, 20
  jump, 76
  nontriviality, 85, 86
  terminal, 87
  transversality
    necessary, 96
    sufficient, 173
Constraint qualification, 30, 86
Constraints
  control, 21, 78
  generalized, 77, 82
  state, 39
    first order, 82
Control
  path, 38, 46, 78
  singular, 109
  variable, 38
Costate
  equation, 82
  function, 76, 84
  system, 130
  trajectory, 102
  variable, 105
Cournot, A., 163
Criterion
  catching up, 95
    sporadically, 95
  overtaking, 95
Cruz, J. B., 102, 105, 108, 125

Decision rules: *see* Loop decision rules
Devil, 18–21, 156, 160
Diffeomorphisms, 59
Differential equations
  autonomous system of
    structurally stable, 32
  matrix-Riccati, 31
Differential games
  exponential, 136
  feedback equivalent, 138
  finite horizon, 37, 38
    description of, 41–43
    normal form of, 49
  generalized, 88
    necessary conditions in, 83–86
    sufficient conditions in, 79, 80, 93, 94
  infinite horizon, 94
  linear-quadratic, 114, 118–121, 123, 124, 128, 129
  open-loop equivalent, 138
  perfect, 113, 138, 139, 141, 147
  qualitatively solvable, 113, 140, 141
  state-redundant, 134, 137, 139, 151
  state-separable, 131, 151
  symmetric, 141, 147
  trilinear, 129–131
  zero-sum, 33
Discontinuity manifolds, 82, 83
Discontinuous feedback rules, 46, 48
  approximation of, 46
Dockner, E., 106, 131, 142
Domain, 82
  decomposition of, 82
Duopoly game, 24
Dynamic programming, 65, 101
  (Hamilton-Jacobi-)Bellman equation of, 65

Eisele, T., 118, 120
Envelope theorem, 63

Equilibria
  of Hamiltonian game, 53, 56, 84
  under hierarchical play
    of Eskimoean game, 107
    for Faust's game, 157
    necessary conditions for, 97–99
    sufficient conditions for, 99–102
  infinite horizon, 95
  "informationally" nonunique, 118
  under simultaneous play: *see* Feedback equilibria, Open-loop equilibria
  subgame perfect, 65–67
  time consistent, 65
Equilibrium, set of actions, 51
Evans, G. C., 163

Faust, 19–21, 49, 54, 156, 159–161
Faust's game, 18–21, 53, 146, 155
Faust legend, 18, 156, 162
Feedback equilibria, 65–68
  necessary conditions for, 55, 56
  for strike negotiation game, 93
  subgame perfect
    for finite horizon oligopoly game, 165
    for infinite horizon oligopoly game, 171
    in linear-quadratic differential games, 120, 121
    in symmetric differential games, 148
  sufficient conditions for, 60, 61, 65, 66

Feichtinger, G., 56, 63, 86, 132, 187
Fershtman, C., 69, 113, 138, 139, 163, 170
Fishery game
  Clemhout and Wan's, 183–186
  competitive limited-access, 25, 106
  Eskimoean, 106–110, 151, 188
  oligopolistic, 179–183
Fleming, W. H., 67
Follower, 96, 97, 124–128
Free (terminal) time problem, 185
Friedman, A., 46, 69, 71
Function
  absolute(ly) continuous, 29
  concave, 30
  piecewise continuous, 31
  piecewise smooth, 31
Fundamental solution, 30

Gale, D., 95
Game
  of capitalism, 21–23, 42, 43, 57–59, 71, 75–77, 81, 82, 110
  finite horizon oligopoly, 164–170
  infinite horizon oligopoly, 170–172
  normal form, 31
  repeated, 32
  zero-sum, 33
  see also Differential games; Metagame
Generalized solution, 48
Goethe, J. W. von, 13, 19, 21, 155
Goethe's (tragedy) "Faust", 19, 160, 162
Gompertz law, 107

Halkin, H., 95
Hamiltonian, 52, 83
  of advertising game, 132
  current value, 149
  extended, 103, 104
  of Faust's game, 53
  game, 53
    transformed, 60
    two-person, 97
  maximizing conditions, 134, 140, 151
  metagame, 54, 109
  transformed, 60, 79
Hardin, G., 32
Harsanyi, J. C., 49, 64
Hartl, R. F., 56, 63, 86
Haurie, A., 70, 101
Hesse, H., 15
Howards, N., 54, 155

Imitator, 175
Information, 42, 43
  pattern of, 41
  set, 28, 65
Initial value problem, 39, 46
Innovator, 174
Intensity
  of research effort, 174
  seducing, 20
  striving, 20
Isaacs, R., 16, 17, 32, 87
Isoclines, 145
  for Faust's game, 146
  for oligopolistic fishery game, 182
  for symmetric differential games, 149

Jacobian (matrix), for Faust's game, 146, 158
Junction points, 84–86

Kamien, M. I., 56, 163, 170, 173
Knowledge, accumulated, 175, 176
Krasovsky, N. N., 46
Kuhn model, 40
Kuhn tree, 30, 42, 65

Lagrangean (function), 83
Lalu, I., 155
Lancaster, K., 21
Lancaster's game of capitalism: *see* Game, of capitalism
Leader, 96, 97, 124, 127, 128
Lebesgue integral, 30
Leitmann, G., 17, 23, 79, 86, 93, 113
Lipschitz condition, 45
Liu, P. T., 23
Loop decision rules (l.d.r.), 40
  induced, 41
  memoryless, 41
  nonanticipative, 40
  open-, 41, 46
  (state) feedback, 41, 46–48
Loop model, 40
Loop representation, 43, 45

Macroeconomic planning, 108
Mäkelä, A., 40
Mapping, induced, 41
Matrix
  negative definite, 31
  negative semidefinite, 31
  rank of, 32
Maximum principle, 31, 56
Mehlmann, A., 19, 113, 137, 139, 187
Mephisto, 19, 20, 49, 54, 156, 160, 161, 162

Metagame, 31
  equilibrium, 99
Mon, G., 17
Morgenstern, C., 153
Morgenstern, O., 16, 155
Moulin, H., 100
Multiplier, 52

Nash, O., 111
Necessary conditions: *see* Equilibria; Feedback equilibria; Stackelberg solutions
Neumann, J. von, 16, 155
Newton, J., 16

Olsder, G. J., 33, 109, 127
Open-loop equilibria
  in finite horizon oligopoly game, 168–170
  in linear-quadratic differential games, 118–120
  subgame perfect
    for advertising game, 134
    for exponential differential game, 136
    for Faust's game, 146
    for game of capitalism, 59
    for qualitatively solvable differential games, 142–144
    for trilinear differential games, 131
Optimal control problem
  leader's, 104
  team, 106
Outcome, 38, 39, 78
  cooperative, 70
  enforceable, 70
  in generalized differential games, 78
  history, 64
Outcome (*cont.*)
  individually-rational, 50
  jointly-rational, 50
  Pareto-efficient, 50, 51, 70, 151
  set, 39, 50
  team optimal, 52

Papavassilopoulos, G. P., 105, 108
Pareto-efficient: *see* Outcome
Patent protection, 178
Payoff, 39, 48
Phase diagram
  analysis, 141–147
    for Faust's game, 146, 147
    for finite horizon oligopoly game, 168–170
    for Goethe's play, 158–160
    for infinite horizon oligopoly game, 172
    for oligopolistic fishery game, 182, 183
    for original Faust legend, 161–162
Pinter, H., 156
Play
  hierarchical, 71
  simultaneous, 42; *see also* Action, simultaneous
  (situation of) extensive, 42
Playable selection, 50, 78
Playing space, 82
Pohjola, M., 108, 110
Pontryagin, L. S., 17, 56
Price
  Cournot equilibrium, 172
  current market, 25, 163
  linear demand, 170
Principle of optimality, 31
Punishment mode, 67

Radner, R., 69
Rapoport, A., 155
Rate
  of advertising expenditures, 131, 132
  concession, 23
  decay
    of market share, 132
  discount, 174, 180
  of fishing effort, 25
  harvest, 180
  hazard, 20, 174
  of production, 24
  revenue, 132
  of seduction, 21, 161
  of time preference, 25
R & D games, 173–178
Reaction
  follower's, 105
    in linear-quadratic differential games, 126
  space of, 54
Reinganum, J. F., 113, 135, 173, 175, 176
Revenue
  marginal, 181
  sale, 184
Rice, G., 35
Rishel, R. W., 67

Saddlepoint, 145
  in finite horizon oligopoly game, 168, 170
  in Goethe's play, 158
  in infinite horizon oligopoly game, 172
  in oligopolistic fishery game, 183
  in original Faust legend, 161
Salvage value, 107
Sarma, I. G., 86
Scherer, F. M., 173
Schmitendorf, W. E., 113
Schwartz, N. L., 56, 173
Security payoff level, 50
Seierstad, A., 56, 86
Selbuz, H., 118
Selten, R., 65
Set
  of actions
    equilibrium, 51
    team optimal, 50
  compact, 47
  of control paths, 38
  convex, 30
  of feedback decision rules, 45
  of loop decision rules, 40
  of open-loop decision rules, 46
  of outcomes: *see* Outcome, set
  of state trajectories, 39
Sethi, S. P., 56
Shakespeare, W., 155
Shubik, M., 164
Simaan, M., 24, 125, 163
Singular surface, 33
"Speed of adjustment", 163
Stability
  global asymptotic, 30, 170
  local asymptotic, 30
  structural: *see* Differential equations, autonomous system of, structurally stable
Stable branch, 168, 170
Stable focus, 145
  in Faust's game, 146
  in Goethe's play, 158
  in original Faust legend, 161
Stable node, 145
Stackelberg solutions, 96

Stackelberg solutions (*cont.*)
  correspondence between metagame equilibria and, 99, 100
  global, 101–103
  at Hamiltonian level, 97–100
  linear, 126
  necessary conditions for, 103–105
  open-loop
    for Eskimoean fishery game, 107, 108
    for linear-quadratic differential games, 124, 125
  stagewise, 101
  subgame perfect, 108
  time consistency of, 105, 106, 108
  time consistent, 108
Stalford, H., 79, 93
State
  initial, 38
  space, 29
    subset of, 59
  terminal, 48
  trajectory, 39
    absolutely continuous, 47; *see also* Generalized solution
  transformation, 139
  variable, 38
    "history dependent", 68, 69
Stationary point, 145
  in Faust's game, 146, 147
  in infinite horizon oligopoly game, 172
  in symmetric differential games, 149
Strategies, 42
Strike negotiation game, 23, 24, 87–93, 109
Subbotin, A., 46
Subdomain, 82, 83, 94
Subgame perfectness, 65, 67, 69
  of open-loop equilibria, 129, 131, 134
Sydsæter, K., 56, 86

Takayama, T., 24, 163
Team
  problem, 32, 118
  solution, 127
  strategy, 127
Tenet of transition, 32
Teodorescu-Brînzeu, P., 155
Terminal time, 80
  points, 88
Thompson, G. L., 56
Threat
  credible, 64
  efficient, 64, 65
  silent, 64, 65
Time consistency: *see* Stackelberg solutions, time consistency of
Tolwinski, B., 69
Tragedy of the commons, 32
Transition line, 32, 87
Tree model, 40; *see also* Kuhn model; Kuhn tree
Trigger strategy combination, 68, 69
Turnpike property, 170

Unstable focus, 145
  in original Faust legend, 161
Unstable node, 145
  in Goethe's play, 158, 159

Vaisbord, E. M., 93
Value
  of Faust's soul, 20, 160

Value (*cont.*)
  function, 136
  of game, 32, 33
Veblen T., 173
Vinci, L. da, 16
Vorobyev, N. N., 156

Wan, H. Y., 113, 129, 148, 183, 186
Weizsäcker, C. C. von, 95
Willing, R., 19, 113, 137, 139

Zaubermann, A., 17
Zhukovsky, Z., 93